Transitions in the Early Years

By the time young children enter statutory education, they may have already attended a number of different educational settings. Entry to group settings outside home, such as playgroup or nursery school, or changes from one setting to another, will involve children in experiences of educational transitions. Each of these experiences is likely to affect children's capacity to adjust and to learn.

This book focuses on children's experiences of personal and curricular transitions in early childhood. The contributors are all academics with international reputations in the field of early childhood education. They draw on their research in Europe and Australasia to consider issues such as:

- the optimum environment and appropriate pedagogy for young children's learning
- how children, parents and educators cope with the transition from home to the first educational settings
- the ways in which professionals can better support and empower children in transition

The perspectives of children, parents and early years educators are all considered and case study examples are used throughout.

This book will be essential reading for anyone involved in working with young children and their families, including students on early years courses, early years practitioners and early years policy makers.

Hilary Fabian is a Lecturer in the Department of Educational Studies, Faculty of Education at the University of Edinburgh.

Aline-Wendy Dunlop is a Senior Lecturer in the Department of Primary Education, Faculty of Education at the University of Strathclyde.

Transitions in the Early Years

Debating continuity and progression for young children in early education

Edited by Hilary Fabian and Aline-Wendy Dunlop

RoutledgeFalmer
Taylor & Francis Group

LONDON AND NEW YORK

First published 2002
by RoutledgeFalmer
2 Park Square, Milton Park, Abingdon, Oxon OX14 4RN

Simultaneously published in the USA and Canada
by RoutledgeFalmer
270 Madison Avenue, New York, NY 10016

Reprinted 2004, 2006

RoutledgeFalmer is an imprint of the Taylor & Francis Group

Typeset in Times by
HWA Text and Data Management, Tunbridge Wells
Printed and bound in Great Britain by
MPG Books Ltd, Bodmin

British Library Cataloguing in Publication Data
A catalogue record for this book is available from the British Library

Library of Congress Cataloging in Publication Data
Transition in the early years : debating continuity and progression for
young children in early education / edited by Hilary Fabian and
Aline-Wendy Dunlop.
    p. cm.
  Includes bibliographical references and index.
    1. Early childhood education. I. Fabian, Hilary. II. Dunlop,
    Aline-Wendy, 1946–

LB1139.23 .T73 2002
372.21–dc21   2002069792

ISBN 0–415–27639–X (HB)
ISBN 0–415–27640–3 (PB)

Contents

Figures

Tables

Contributors

Professor Stig Broström is Associate Professor in Early Childhood Education at The Danish University of Education in Copenhagen. Since 1969 he has been involved in the field of early years education. Thus he has a long experience in this area, both as a pre-school teacher, teacher at a college for pre-school teachers, and as teacher and researcher at The Danish University of Education. His main areas of research are related to children's life in pre-school and kindergarten with the focus on children's play, social competence and friendship. His PhD thesis, an ethnographic and comparative study, deals with transition issues exposed through children's social competence and learning motivation in Danish and American classrooms. Currently he is involved with a research programme that focuses on the development of a curriculum for the early years, and that reflects the transition theme.

Dr Carmen Dalli is Senior Lecturer and Director of the Institute for Early Childhood Studies at Victoria University of Wellington, New Zealand where she has taught since 1988. She is also director of the BEd (Teaching) Early Childhood programme, which Victoria University jointly awards with the Wellington College of Education. She teaches undergraduate and postgraduate courses in early childhood studies and is also strongly involved in in-service professional development for early childhood educators. Dr Dalli was part of the national working group that developed the early childhood code of ethics for Aotearoa, New Zealand. She retains an interest in how the code is used by the sector and her research interests include professionalism and ethical practice in early childhood, as well as young children's development and early childhood education policy. Recently she completed a qualitative case study project that explored the experience of starting childcare from the perspective of children, parents and early childhood teachers. She has been a primary and secondary school teacher, but has been working in early childhood for the past sixteen years.

Aline-Wendy Dunlop has taught in the university sector since 1993: first at Moray House Institute of Education in Edinburgh and currently at the University of Strathclyde where she is a senior lecturer and course director of two postgraduate programmes: Early Education, and Autism, she is also a doctoral student. Her very varied teaching experience over 23 years in schools and the community includes home visiting, training education staff in residential childcare, teaching SNNEB students, working with parents, special educational needs and mainstream early education and has made her aware of the many different transitions which young children and those closest to them may go through. Her main areas of current research interest are leadership in early education, special needs, social interaction, the empowerment of families of very young children and continuity and progression for children in educational transitions.

Dr Hilary Fabian has worked in the field of early years education since 1970 and is currently teaching at the University of Edinburgh on the BEd, PGCE and SQH programmes. She has taught young children in the London Boroughs of Hillingdon and Harrow, with the Service Children's Education Authority in Germany, and in Buckinghamshire and Shropshire. From 1991 to 2000 she was a senior lecturer at the Manchester Metropolitan University where she was course leader for the Early Years Continuing Professional Development programmes. She has been a NPQH assessor, a Registered Nursery Inspector and education consultant for the British Forces 'Counterpoint' radio programme. Her master's and her PhD theses, journal publications, and book *Children Starting School*, reflect her interest in the transitions that people make in their lives and the management of their induction to new situations.

Dr Jan Fortune-Wood read theology at Cambridge and completed her PhD in the relationship of feminist Christology to church structures. She currently works as a parish priest in Birmingham and has a considerable interest in, and experience of, assisting people to make successful life transitions. She has worked as a teacher in secondary education in Bristol and with a number of agencies supporting parents and young children. She has recently set up a local community charity working with parents and children under stress. She educates her four children at home with her husband and has published two books with Educational Heretics Press – *Doing It Their Way: Home Based Education and Autonomous Learning* and *Without Boundaries: Consent Based, Non-coercive Parenting and Autonomous Learning*.

Wilfried Griebel (Diplom-Psych.) has worked as a member of the scientific staff of the State Institute for Early Childhood Pedagogic and Research, Munich, Germany, and its director, Prof. Dr. W. E. Fthenakis since 1982. In his research on families he has explored the role of fathers in different family structures. As a psychological expert he dealt with cases of custody and access, has trained social workers, counsellors, judges and others, on families in divorce, stepfamilies, foster families, and families with adopted children. Together with Professor Fthenakis and other colleagues, he has published on these topics. The work of the Staatsinstitut für Frühpädagogik (IFP) State Institute of Early

Childhood Education and Research) on joint custody and post-divorce parental co-operation helped to evolve practise of social work, jurisdiction and finally legislation, when in Germany in 1998 a new law on the child's family relationships after separation and divorce was passed. His work on interactions between family and institutions, and especially the study on transition from kindergarten to school, undertaken together with Renate Niesel, is part of development of a new national curriculum which emphasises coping with transitions.

Research Director Inge Johansson has worked for the last 25 years in research in the field of linkages between school, preschool, recreational centres and the local community. He is primarily interested in the development of knowledge and learning in new institutions which integrate school, preschool and recreational centre under one roof. He is currently Research Director for the 'Children, Youth and School' in the city of Stockholm, Sweden. He has been Professor in Pedagogy focused on child research at the University of Linkoping, Sweden.

Dr Anna Kienig is Senior Lecturer of Developmental Psychology and Early Education at the University of Białstok, in the Faculty of Pedagogy and Psychology, Department of Early Childhood Education. She has taught at the University of Białstok for the last twenty years in the field of early years education. She is Course Leader for the post-diploma programme 'Child Development Support in the Early Years'. Her research interest is in child development, particularly developmental disharmonies and social development. This encompasses transitions in the early years and connections between the process of early adjustment to new settings and later social behaviour. She is editor of *Nowy Test* (*The Journal of Psychology and Education*). She is a member of the European Early Childhood Education Research Association and the Society for Research in Child Development (USA).

Dr Kay Margetts is Lecturer in Early Childhood Studies, Faculty of Education, The University of Melbourne. Prior to this she was lecturer in Child Development and Special Needs at Monash University, Project Officer – in-service and Professional Development Programmes at the Lady Gowrie Child Centre, writer and producer of children's television programmes, and a preschool teacher working in both sessional and long day programmes. Her research interests focus on early childhood development and practice with a particular focus on children's adjustment in the first year of schooling. She has presented papers at national and international conferences and has a good record of publications. She regularly provides professional development and consultancy to early childhood personnel from a range of sectors including preschool services and the early years of schooling.

Michelle J. Neuman is a Graduate Research Fellow at the Center for Children and Families at Teachers College, Columbia University where she is also a doctoral student. Between 1997 and 2001, she was the Project Leader for the OECD Thematic Review of Early Childhood Education and Care Policy, a comparative study in twelve countries. She developed the proposal for the study, the framework for analysis, and the questions for investigation. As part of the study, she led teams of experts on visits to the twelve countries to review their early childhood policies. She co-authored the 2001 OECD comparative report, *Starting Strong: Early Childhood Education and Care*. She previously worked at the Yale Bush Center in Child Development and Social Policy, where her research and writing focused on policy areas related to young children and their families. She is a graduate of the Woodrow Wilson School of Public and International Affairs at Princeton University.

Renate Niesel (Diplom-Psych.) is a member of the scientific staff of the State Institute of Childhood Education and Research in Munich, Germany. She started her work on transitions in the field of family research understanding divorce as a transitional process demanding complex adaptations and coping strategies from parents and children. She was co-author of expert statements and publications that led to changes in custody laws and child welfare practice. Transferring her experience from family research to early childhood education she carried out empirical studies together with Wilfried Griebel on the transition from family to kindergarten and from kindergarten to school in Bavaria. She also works as a lecturer for kindergarten and schoolteachers on in-service courses and undergraduate students of early childhood education.

Sally Peters is a lecturer at the University of Waikato, teaching and coordinating courses on human development and inclusive education. Prior to this she taught at the Institute for Early Childhood Studies, Victoria University of Wellington. She has a background in early childhood education and is involved in research that explores the experiences of children, parents and teachers during the transition to school. Her other research interests include children's thinking, especially the development of mathematical thinking. She was a member of the Minister of Education's policy advisory group for the New Zealand early childhood curriculum *Te Whaariki* and has contributed to the Ministry of Education's 'Feed the Mind' campaign.

Foreword

This book appears at a significant time for those who work in early childhood education. Many governments are seeking to expand the availability of services for young children. One result of these initiatives is that across the world children are entering institutionalised care and education at an ever earlier age and for an increasingly extended period of their young lives. The evidence suggests that the experiences of children in their early years are critical determinants of future progress and attainment educationally, economically and as a member of their social community. These changing contexts place a burden of responsibility on those who provide early childhood services to ensure that they benefit rather than damage children's potential. This means paying serious attention to ensuring the quality of experience for the child as they transfer across an increasing number of settings in their early years.

Alongside this refocusing of attention on the development of coherent, high quality services for children from birth has been a growing acknowledgement of Children's Rights. This adds weight to the current emphasis on developing children's autonomy and ability to act as an agent of their own destiny. Despite the lack of serious study of the politics of childhood, the requirement that services empower children by viewing them as competent and powerful actors in their own narratives of life is a welcome theme in more recent developments of educational provision.

These changes in political and social thinking are part of the dynamic of change that is a dominant characteristic of modern life. The pace and number of changes that we all have to manage has increased phenomenally over recent years. These changes are both structural and qualitative and affect almost every domain of daily life. Young children, from birth, are living in an unpredictable world where change and discontinuity may be all that they can be sure of, and in which the transitions they are having to make, are numerous. Until recently there has been hardly any acknowledgement of the professional and personal challenges that this context of continuous transitions provides for those concerned with the quality of experience for the child. The intervention programmes available for practitioners to help young children cope with transitions and capitalise on the opportunities they bring have been rare and underdeveloped. This book is important because it demonstrates an increasing international acknowledgement of the universality of the challenges of managing transitions effectively, and as such it is timely and enormously helpful.

The group of academics who have collaborated to produce this edited book are all senior and respected researchers, writers and activists in the field of early childhood in their respective countries. They have come together as a special interest group focused on transitions through their involvement in the European Early Childhood Education Research Association (EECERA). As such they demonstrate the benefits of sharing common problems and expertise in developing reflective practice at an international level. They also exemplify their Association's concern to bring together theory, research and practice in a powerful and convincing account of the salient issues concerned with continuity and progression as children make their transitions through the many social environments and experiences that now make up a child's early life. The blend of scholarship and practice, and the rigour of the research in the writing contained in this book is a model for others to follow. They have succeeded in making this expert knowledge accessible and directly relevant to those concerned with developing the quality of policy and practice in the field. Their joint work on transitions will make an important contribution to ensuring our young children negotiate the challenges of their twenty-first century lives with their competencies and confidence enhanced and their ability to cope with the known and the unknown undaunted.

Professor Christine Pascal

Acknowledgements

The authors are indebted to the European Early Childhood Education Association for the opportunities it has afforded them to meet and present their work together at several of their annual conferences. This book has come about largely through the debate and discussion at these events.

Australia

	Name of setting	Education: E Care/social welfare: C	Number of children in a class/group	Name of curriculum document or government guidance	Job title of staff involved	Hours of attendance	Other centres this age may attend	Staff:child ratios
Under 3 years	Long day care, child care or centre-based child care	C/E	Up to 20, varies with age and regulations	Quality Implementation and Accreditation System Curriculum documents vary from state to state	Child care worker Coordinator	Up to 50 hours per week Up to 8 hours per day	Family daycare	Varies between states 1:4 or 1:5
3–4 years	Kindergarten or pre-school	E	Up to 25/30	Regulations and curriculum documents vary from state to state	Teacher Director Assistant	4–10 hours per week 2–3 hours per day	Family daycare Occasional care Centre-based	Varies 1:10, 1:10 or 1:24
	Childcare	C/E	15 to 30	As for under 3 years	Child care worker Coordinator	Up to 50 hours per week		As above
4–5 years	Kindergarten or pre-school	E	Up to 30	As for 3–4 year olds	Teacher Director Assistant	10–12.5 hours 2–5 hours per day	Centre-based care Family daycare Occasional care	As above
5–6 years	In some sates pre-school is free Fees paid for care of children under school age sub-sidised.**	E	20–30	State Curriculum Guidelines of Standards	Teacher	Up to 32.5 hours per week	Centre-based child care Family daycare Occasional care Pre-school kindergarten pre-prep transition	Again this varies but may be as high as 1:30

						Outside school hours care	I teacher per class
School	E	Up to 30	As above	Teacher	32.5 hours per week 6.5 hours per day		I teacher per class
6–7 years	Children are usually in school by the age of 6 years	E	Up to 30		Teacher		I teacher per class
Over 7 years	E	Up to 30		Teacher			I teacher per class

* Some children attend more formal school-focused programmes – pre-prep pre-kindergarten transition, where the guidelines vary with the setting. ** In Victoria all children are entitled to one year of subsidised pre-school.

Denmark

	Name of setting	Education: E Care/social welfare: C	Numbers of children in a class/group	Name of curriculum document or government guidance	Job title of staff involved	Hours of attendance	Other centres this age may attend
Under 3 years	Crèche	E/C	8–12 children	Social Services Act	Pedagogue	9–11 hours	Private child minding (organised by the municipality)
3–4 years	Day care centre/kindergarten	E/C	20 children	Social Services Act	Pedagogue	9–11 hours	Private child minding (organised by the municipality)
4–5 years	Day care centre/kindergarten	E/C	20 children	Social Services Act	Pedagogue	9–11 hours	Private child minding (organised by the municipality)
5–6 years	Day care centre/kindergarten	E/C	20 children	Social Services Act	Pedagogue	9–11 hours	Private child minding (organised by the municipality)
6–7 years	Kindergarten class (in school) and leisure-time centre	E/C	20 children	Social Services Act	Pedagogue	9–11 hours	Private child minding (organised by the municipality)
Over 7 years	Over 7: school and leisure-time centre	E/C	In school grade 1 up to 27 children. Leisure-time centre 20 children (or more)	Folk School Act	In school: teacher. At leisure-time centre: pedagogue	9–11 hours	Private child minding (organised by the municipality) plus different kinds of clubs

Pre-school: two to three adults to 20 children. As a rule two of them are qualified. Kindergartem class: generally there is 1 pedagogue (qualified adult) per class. Usually there are 20 children per class, however there can be as many as 27. In some municipalities there is also a helper (non-qualified) attached to the class (or on extra adult attached to 2 kindergarten classes). Leisure time centre: 1 qualified pedagogue tp 15.52 children.

England

Age	Name of setting	Education: E Care/social welfare: C	Numbers of children in a class/group	Name of curriculum document or government guidance	Job title of staff involved	Hours of attendance	Other centres this age may attend
Under 3 years	Pre-school nursery	C/E			Nursery nurse	Typically: 9.00 am–4.00 pm	
3–4 years	Pre-school nursery	C/E	1:10	Foundation Stage: Early Learning Goals	Nursery nurse	Typically: 9.00 am–4.00 pm	
4–5 years	Infant school reception class	E	1:30	Foundation Stage: Early Learning Goals	Teacher	Typically: 9.00 am–3.15 pm	Wraparound care, out-of-school-hours-learning
5–6 years	Infant school year 1	E	1:30	National Curriculum: Key Stage 1	Teacher	Typically: 9.00 am–3.15 pm	
6–7 years	Infant school year 2	E	1:30	National Curriculum: Key Stage 1	Teacher	Typically: 9.00 am–3.15 pm	
Over 7 years	Junior school	E	1:30+	National Curriculum: Key Stage 2	Teacher	Typically: 9.00 am–3.30 pm	

Germany

	Name of setting	Education: E Care/social welfare: C	Numbers of children in a class/group	Name of curriculum document or government guidance	Job title of staff involved	Hours of attendance	Other centres this age may attend
Under 3 years	Krippe (crèche)	C	6–8	SGB VIII*	Erzieherin (educator)	4–8	Day mother, mixed age group
3–4 years	Kindergarten (nursery school)	C/E	15–30	As above	Erzieherin	4–8	Day mother, mixed age group
4–5 years	Kindergarten	C/E	15–30	As above	Erzieherin	4–8	Day mother, mixed age group
5–6 years	Kindergarten	C/E	15–30	As above	Erzieherin	4–8	Day mother, mixed age group
6–7 years	School	E	20–35	Lehrplan (defined curriculum)	Lehrer Lehrerin (teacher)	4–5	Ganztags-Schule (all-day school), Hort (afternoon day-care for pupils), mixed age group
Over 7 years	School	E	20–35	Lehrplan	Lehrer, Lehrerin	4–5	Ganztags-Schule, Hort, mixed age group

* 8th volume of the Social Welfare Legislation (Sozialgesetzbuch – Kinder und Jugendhilfe (SGB VIII)) as well as implementation of states' regulation on childcare. All kinds of daycare outside school (crèche, day mother, nursery school, afternoon daycare for pupils) has to be paid for.

New Zealand

	Name of setting	Education: E Care/social welfare: C	Numbers of children in a class/group	Name of curriculum document or government guidance	Job title of staff involved	Hours of attendance	Other centres this age may attend
Under 3 years	Playcentre Kohanga Reo Licensed childcare centres Family daycare Pacific Island language groups Community playgroups Some kindergartens	E	No more than 25 children under two, no more than 50 over two, but usually fewer than this. Family daycare groups: no more than 4 under-6s and no more than 2 under-2s	Curriculum: Te Whaariki. Education (Early Childhood Centres) Regulations 1998. Education (Home-based Care) Order 1992; amended 1998.	Educator Teacher Kaiako	All day (more than 4 hours) or sessional (less than 4 hours per day depending on the type of service and family requirements	
3–4 years	As above, plus Kindergarten Correspondence School	E	No more than 50 children, but usually fewer than this*	As above	Educator Teacher Kaiako	As above	
4–5 years	As for 3–4 years	E	As above	As above	Educator Teacher Kaiako		
5–6 years	Most 5 year olds and all 6 year olds attend primary school	E	Early childhood services: as above School: staffed 1:23 or 1:27 but class sizes vary	Early childhood: Te Whaariki School: NZ Curriculum Framework	Teacher Kaiako	Early childhood services: as above School: 6 hours	Home schooling
6–7 years	Primary School	E	1:23 or 1:27, class sizes vary	NZ Curriculum Framework	Teacher Kaiako	6 hours	As above
Over 7 years	Primary School	E	1:29 or 1:27 class sizes vary.	NZ Curriculum Framework	Teacher Kaiako	6 hours	As above

* Regulated ratios may vary by age of child, mix of ages in a centre and by whether a centre is full day or sessional. Ratios range from 1 adult to 3 children in a full-day mixed age centre to 4 adults to 50 children in a sessional centre for over 2-year-olds.

Note: Attendance at kindergarten is free though donations are sought. Parents and government share the cost of all other early childhood services on an approximate 50:50 basis.

Poland

	Name of setting	Education: E Care/social welfare: C	Numbers of children in a class/group	Name of curriculum document or government guidance	Job title of staff involved	Hours of attendance	Other centres this age may attend
Under 3 years	1. Żłobek (nursery) 2. Przedskole (pre-school centre)	1. C 2. E	15–20		Nurse Pre-school teacher	7–17	
3–4 years	Przedskole (pre-school centre)	E	25	Basic Curriculum of Pre-school Education (2000)	Pre-school teacher	7–17	
4–5 years	Przedskole (pre-school centre)	E	25	As above	Pre-school teacher	7–17	
5–6 years	Przedskole (pre-school centre)	E	25	As above	Pre-school teacher	7–17	
6–7 years	1. Przedskole (pre-school centre) 2. Oddział prezedskolny w szkole (class O)	E	25	Basic	Pre-school teacher Teacher	7–17	
Over 7 years	Szkoła	E	22–30	Basic Curriculum of Primary Education (1999)	Teacher	8–12	

Scotland

	Name of setting	Education: E Care/social welfare: C	Numbers of children in a class/group	Name of curriculum document or government guidance	Job title of staff involved	Hours of attendance	Other centres this age may attend
Under 3 years	Nursery	C or private	Under 1: 1:3 1–2 years: 1:5 2–3 years: 1:8	Local documentation in some areas	Nursery nurse	Opening hours: 7.30 am–6.00 pm: attendance varies	Parent and toddler groups; playgroups
3–4 years	Early years setting: pre-school or nursery	E Childcare partnerships managed by local authority	1:10	A Curriculum Framework for Children 3–5: Scottish National document	Teacher assisted by nursery nurse	Usually 2.5–3 part-time sessions morning of afternoon 2.5–3 hour 9.00–12.00 am or 1.00–4.00 pm	Wrap around care to complement nursery hours
4–5 years	Early years setting: pre-school or nursery	E Childcare partnerships managed by local authority	1:10	As above	Teacher assisted by nursery nurse	As above	Wrap around care as above
5–6 years	Primary school: Primary 1	E	1:30	Scottish 5–14 Curriculum and Assessment in Scotland: National Guidelines	Teacher and sometimes classroom assistants	Usually 9.00 – 3.15 pm	After school clubs
6–7 years	Primary School: Primary 2	E	1:30	Scottish 5–14 Curriculum Guidelines	Teacher and sometimes classroom assistants	9.00 am – 3.15 pm	After school clubs
Over 7 years	Primary school	E	Maximum 33	Scottish 5–14 Curriculum Guidelines	Teacher	9.00 am – 3.30 pm	After school clubs

Sweden

	Name of setting	Education: E Care/social welfare: C	Numbers of children in a class/group	Name of curriculum document or government guidance	Job title of staff involved	Hours of attendance	Other centres this age may attend
Under 3 years	Pre-school	E	Not available National figures	National Curriculum for the pre-school	Pre-school teacher, day care nurse, childminder	Approx. 29 hours per week	Family day nursery
3–4 years	Pre-school	E			Pre-school teacher, day care nurse, childminder	31 hours per week	Family day nursery
4–5 years	Pre-school	E			Pre-school teacher, day care nurse, childminder	31 hours per week	Family day nursery
5–6 years	Pre-school	E			Pre-school teacher, day care nurse, childminder	31 hours per week	Family day nursery
6–7 years	Pre-school class/school age child care	E		National Curriculum for the Compulsory School	Pre-school teacher, recreational pedagogue, school teacher	Approx. 30 hours per week (incl school age child care	Family day nursery
Over 7 years	School class/school age child care	E		National Curriculum for the Compulsory School	Recreational pedagogue, school teacher	Approx. 30 hours per week	Kids clubs etc.

Introduction

Hilary Fabian and Aline-Wendy Dunlop

At a time when young children are likely to have experience of many different transitions both educationally and in their family lives, there is more emphasis on an earlier start in group day-care and educational settings than ever before. By the time children enter statutory education they may have already attended a number of educational settings. Each of these experiences is likely to affect children and their capacity to adjust and to learn. Such is the significance of early transitions for young children that it is essential that parents, educators, policy makers and politicians pay close attention to young children's experiences in order to provide well for them. Recently there has been an increase in the demand for early years education in the countries that are the subject of this book. Expansion of early education has led to an increase in the number of moves that young children experience and awareness by practitioners of the need to address the issues surrounding transitions. Expansion of early education, the nature of the curriculum and the dominance of an 'early start' raise issues of differing perspectives on what is important for young children: legislation on children's rights demands that children have a chance to express a view; parents have a right of choice in deciding their child's schooling; and educators are expected to meet the requirements of the curriculum. We ask whether varied perspectives matter; what is the optimum environment and appropriate pedagogy for young children's learning; how are the transitions experienced for parents, educators and the children themselves as they move from home to the various educational settings in which they find themselves; and whether there are ways in which adults can better support and empower children in transition. We find that these are international issues although there are cultural differences in the ages of transition, provision and curriculum ideology.

Many early childhood publications touch on issues of transition, continuity and progression. Such words appear in any good index, but this book brings together new ideas and theories about transition and gives it, in a single volume, the serious attention that it merits. This book aims to bring attention to children's experiences of personal and curricular transitions in early childhood from entry to group-settings outside home to joining playgroup or nursery school and on into the early years of formal education. The perspectives of children, parents and early educators are all considered.

Each of the chapters is informed by rigorous research. The authors have all presented publicly and successfully at home and abroad and have published in academic journals. They are all academics with international reputations in the field of early childhood education. Most have experience of teacher education and continuing professional development for early childhood professionals and all share an interest in issues of transition, continuity and progression for young children in their early education. These are key elements in children's school success and have a high profile on government agendas across the world. Sharing our work through publication and presentation, particularly at EECERA conferences on Quality in Early Childhood Education, has contributed to the development of our individual work and to a heightened awareness of the lasting significance of transitions for young children and their families nationally and internationally.

A conceptual framework for transitions

The structure of the book includes historical perspectives, curriculum interpretations, current practice in the management of transitions, a range of perspectives about the notion of transition and the transition itself, the wider socio-cultural influences on transition, empowerment of children and intervention for change. The following grid shows the different themes and elements that are addressed and that inform transitions:

		Culture		
Home	Children	Relationships	Responsibility	Programmes
Pre-school	Parents	Contexts for learning/pedagogy	Policy	Reorganisation/ Intervention
School	Teachers	Curriculum	Wider influences	Empowerment Information

The epistemological elements are inter-linked, knitted together and difficult to separate. They are informed by Bronfenbrenner's (1979) portrayal of the developing child as being at the centre of an interconnected set of contexts or microsystems. These are interrelated with, and affected by, other systems that influence the developing person and are 'nested' like a Russian doll one within the other. Transitions are influenced by cultural ideas of childhood such as the age at which the family and the welfare system expect children to enter, and progress through, the education system. Each new phase in this progression brings a re-organisation of roles for children and their parents that can cause strong emotions and possible disharmony. Each new context brings a change in the nature and behaviour of the child, as children's learning and development is not context-free. In each setting there is a culture present that needs to be understood to give the setting meaning. This culture represents the shared values, traditions and beliefs characteristic of the setting. Bruner (1996) suggests that participation in the culture helps understanding of that culture and shapes the mind towards adapting and acquiring the ways of thinking in that setting. The theoretical strands bridge the sociological and psychological disciplines permeating throughout the book and are used to explain aspects and processes of transition.

For the purposes of this book, the word 'transition' is referred to as the process of change that is experienced when children (and their families) move from one setting to another. For example, when a child moves from home to pre-school, or from pre-school to school. It includes the length of time it takes to make such a change, spanning the time between any pre-entry visit(s) and settling-in, to when the child is more fully established as a member of the new setting. It is usually a time of intense and accelerated developmental demands that are socially regulated.

We place emphasis on continuity of children's experiences and on making transitions seamless. The book highlights some of the discontinuities that are experienced as children move from one setting to another. These include physical, social and philosophical discontinuities that often impact on the emotional well-being of children and can impede learning. Progression in learning is another strand that occurs throughout the book and is explored from a number of perspectives.

The chapters follow a logical sequence. They encompass themes for children's success in day-to-day matters and social integration, and acknowledge that learning is influenced by the nature of the transition and that there are certain factors that contribute to this. The themes and elements are broad and are addressed implicitly in all the writing. Therefore the book is not a comparative review: rather, each chapter makes a unique contribution that highlights a specific aspect of transition and can be read as a single unit, sequentially or as part of a group. For example Margetts, Broström and Fabian's chapters make a set about strategies, whilst Dalli, Greibel and Niesel, and Dunlop's each look at perspective in different ways, as does a different grouping of Keinig, Johansson, and Peters.

The chapters

Michelle Neuman begins the book by drawing on the recently completed OECD thematic review of early childhood education and care (ECEC) policy to frame children's transitions in the wider context of cross-national developments in early childhood policies and provision. She discusses how the twelve countries in the review are expanding provision toward universal access, raising the quality of provision, promoting coherence, co-ordinating policy and services, and ensuring adequate investment in the system. After this overview, the chapter focuses more specifically on transition issues. At what age do children make the transition from home to ECEC, and from ECEC to school in OECD countries? What are some of the barriers to developing smooth transitions? How are countries promoting links between home and ECEC and ECEC and schools? The chapter provides examples of strategies to facilitate transitions in four main areas: (1) structural continuity; (2) pedagogical and programme continuity; (3) professional continuity; and (4) continuity with the home and community. The chapter argues that it is important to develop a systematic and integrated approach to early childhood policy development – including a strong and equal partnership with the education system – in order to promote coherence and smooth transitions for children and their families.

Anna Kienig explores some of the developmental disharmonies in transition found in Poland and emphasises that the beginning of pre-school education can be a time when worrying examples of children's behaviour can be seen. Many children have problems with adjustment to the new environment and present behaviour disorders during entry to educational settings. The process of adjustment requires meeting the demands of two environments: the family and the educational setting. The differences between the requirements established by these two settings can create problems related to adjustment that may result in disturbances of children's later development. Anna argues that this adjustment can influence the ability of the child to function in other environments and might create serious problems in the further social adjustment of children to other settings. The process of adjustment during early transitions, therefore, forms a pattern for further transitions with the consequences of adjustment disorders in early childhood having a long-term influence.

Carmen Dalli looks at very young children's and their parents' transition to day-care. She argues that, to date, research on starting childcare has focused too narrowly on children's experiences, and within this, too narrowly on this experience as one of separation. This chapter shows that when one adopts a multiple perspective on the lived experience of starting childcare, this event emerges as a complex experience which poses challenges for all involved: children, parents and centre adults. The chapter discusses these challenges using findings from a case study project carried out in five different New Zealand childcare centres. The study explored how starting childcare was experienced by five under-three-year-old children, their mothers and at least one teacher in the childcare centre attended by the children. Using data from interviews with adults, the adults' journal records and observational field notes of the children's experiences, including video records, narratives of the experiences of each group of participants were created. The chapter illustrates the complexity of these experiences including the balancing of conflicting emotions by the mothers, the influences on the teachers' practice during this time, and what the children learned during this first transition from home to an educational setting. Some implications of this study for enhancing the starting childcare experience are discussed.

Stig Broström looks at the transition from kindergarten to school in Denmark. He identifies new research on children's expectations of school which shows their lack of insight into what will happen in school. Moreover, a substantial group of children have an outdated picture of the school as a place where they sit down and behave quietly, or else they are scolded and smacked by the teacher. Further to this, there are enormous educational contradictions between kindergarten and school. Common practice in kindergarten stresses play, and creative-aesthetic activities with teachers in a supporting role. New research shows that in school the emphasis is on teaching, learning and the curriculum, especially reading and writing activities, leading to teachers claiming that children lack skills and competence. The criticism is that kindergarten does not contribute to a level of development necessary for children being able to make use of the learning environment in school. In other words, too many children do not obtain a level of school readiness.

The problems described advocate the establishment of transition activities to ensure continuity in children's lives. This implies that parents, pre-school teachers, teachers, and leisure time teachers need to work in close co-operation. New research shows that such developed relationships and communication are the pivot for a good start in school and the concept of the 'child-ready school' is introduced. Further, new research indicates that teachers are ready to establish transition practices. This chapter deals with the description of some of those different transition activities.

Wilfried Griebel and Renate Niesel summarise some of the results of two empirical studies carried out in Bavaria, Germany, exploring transitions from the perspective of the children. The theoretical background is a multi-perspective transition approach to family development where transition is understood as a process leading to changes in identity, roles and relationships, and where transition processes often evoke strong emotions and stress.

Results very clearly show differences between the perspective of professionals' routines and the unique experience of children and parents. Although kindergarten and schoolteachers' experiences are very demanding in guiding children and parents into kindergarten and school, they do not experience a transition themselves. This chapter discusses the pedagogical task of supporting the coping with transition and its challenging nature.

Parents and educators need to enter a dialogue about pedagogical concepts, about what is done and not done in the institution and in the family to prepare children to cope with the transition to school. Parents' expectations, as well as their fears and hopes, influence the children's perspective through verbal and non-verbal messages. Preparation for school, therefore, is needed not only for children, but also for parents. Part of this chapter has as its focus, transitions in children, and families' lives in general as well as inter-institutional transitions that need to be understood by educators and teachers.

Inge Johansson looks at the influence of parents on transitions for children and takes account of school reform in Sweden, which itself is going through a transition. He highlights that the transition from pre-school to school is a crucial period for a child in that the first contact with school is of vital importance in how the child will experience school as an arena for learning and social development in the future. Results from research have shown that the support from the parents and how they regard the transition are very influential on how the child adjusts to the new situation. In a research project the parents´ view of their children's transition and how they look upon the first period in school have been studied. In this chapter results from this study are presented and discussed. Two aspects that have impact here are the engagement of parents and their level of involvement in actively choosing a school for their child.

Sally Peters explores teachers' perspectives in New Zealand. She notes that teachers' views of their roles in facilitating the transition to school vary both within and across the early childhood and school sectors. She suggests that consideration of teachers' perspectives of transition serve to highlight some of the pedagogical issues in early years education and the tensions teachers face in meeting the competing demands of their role. Exploring the complexity of these issues is an important step in developing policies and practices that enhance the transition experiences of children and their families.

Aline-Wendy Dunlop looks at differing views in Scotland about children as learners and the influence this might have on the success of a transition. It is widely accepted that the passage through major changes in our lives can have lasting effects on how we see ourselves, the value we feel others place on us, our sense of well-being and consequently how we are able to learn. One of the major differences that children meet as they move settings from home to pre-school to school education is likely to be the way in which they are seen as learners. Different views of children as learners, including the children's own, may have implications for, and shed some light on, why some children find such transitions easier than others. Their ability to claim the new setting as their own and to benefit educationally from it may be reflected in the degree to which their educators have collaborated in a shared conceptual framework of children's learning. This chapter asks what are children like as learners, and whether or not educators' views of pre-school and primary children differ.

Kay Margetts looks at some practical strategies from Australia that can support children and involve their parents in the transition to school. Children entering school face a setting that is qualitatively different from their pre-school experience in terms of the curriculum, the setting and the people. There is concern that these differences may impact on children's adjustment to school, and disrupt their learning and developmental processes. When children adjust adequately in the first year of school, much of the initial stress associated with transition can be overcome, and children are more likely to be successful in their future progress than children who have difficulty adjusting to the new situation. The impact and stress associated with transition to school are being recognised by many teachers and transition programmes are being implemented to minimise the adjustments required for successful transition into the first year of school.

This chapter identifies the challenges facing children as they commence school and explores strategies for creating an appropriate degree of continuity between pre-school and school experiences. Issues associated with important elements for successful transition are presented including the preparation of children for school, the involvement of parents in the transition, and communication and collaboration between early childhood services and schools.

Hilary Fabian's research in England found that although most children look forward to the start of school, many also worry about the physical and social environment that they may come across. Children need to make sense of school with its institutional ways, a bewildering number of unfamiliar words and a strange culture if they are going to be happy and learn. This chapter explores one way of empowering children with coping skills for the transition to school, giving them an understanding of the nature of school and helping them develop some social and emotional resilience in dealing with new situations. Influenced by the work of Bruner, it looks at ways in which teachers can help children settle into school through stories that focus on critical incidents and every day situations common to school. These are used to raise questions about school processes and to help children find solutions to situations that they may meet at school, thus enabling children to deal with unfamiliar situations and develop their thinking skills.

Jan Fortune-Wood takes a very different perspective and explores education without overt transitions. The management of transitions is a major learning experience for school-going children, but an increasing number of parents and their children question the need for, and role of, school in life transitions. For home-educated children, transitions are intrinsically motivated and made within a consistent environment, with consistent adult helpers. The chapter explores the role of self-motivation in developing resourcefulness, self-reliance and autonomous identity and asks whether home education is a help or a hindrance to children in developing maturity and independence. The chapter explores autonomy as an assumption fundamental to the learning process, rather than as a goal of transitions and considers how home educated children can develop the skills of coping with unfamiliar circumstances and the demands of differing environments. The role of socialisation is considered and home educating parents express their opinions on how their children make successful transitions without school.

References

Bronfenbrenner, U. (1979) *The Ecology of Human development: Experiments by Nature and Design.* Massachusetts: Harvard University Press.

Bruner, J.S. (1996) *The Culture of Education.* Massachusetts: Harvard University Press.

Chapter 1

The wider context

An international overview of transition issues

Michelle J. Neuman

The OECD has documented an unprecedented surge of international policy attention to the early years of children's lives (OECD, 2001). Policymakers are recognising the importance of quality early childhood education and care (ECEC) provision for children's short-term and long-term well being, as well as an essential tool to support working parents. Increasingly, ECEC is being viewed also as a tool for social integration. Over the past five years, countries have expanded provision toward universal access, raised the quality of provision, and increased investment in the system. Growing international attention to ECEC has generated increased awareness of the importance of providing continuity and coherence in children's early development and learning. Drawing on the findings of the OECD thematic review of early childhood education and care policy (OECD, 2001) in twelve countries[1], this chapter will frame children's transitions within the wider context of the cross-national development of early childhood policies and provision: How coherent are children's early childhood experiences? At what age do children make the transition to ECEC and from ECEC to school in OECD countries? What are some of the barriers to developing smooth transitions? What are some promising strategies to promote links between home and ECEC and between ECEC and schools? The chapter provides diverse country examples to illustrate approaches to facilitating transitions in four main areas: (1) structural continuity; (2) pedagogical and programme continuity; (3) professional continuity; and (4) continuity with the home.

Main transition issues

Within the context of expansion and improvement of ECEC policy and provision, there has been growing attention to the coherence of children's early development and learning on a given day and over time. Children may experience several *vertical* transitions – e.g. when they move from home to ECEC, from one ECEC setting to another as they get older, or from home or ECEC to primary school. In addition, children may also experience *horizontal* transitions in the early years, those which occur during a given day (Kagan, 1991). Children attending part-day (e.g. play groups and some nursery provision) or school-based programmes – which do not cover their parents' work day – may experience horizontal transitions to another form of ECEC, perhaps out-of-school or leisure-time provision. Children with disabilities may face another kind of *horizontal* transition – the transition from special services to mainstream classrooms. Just as there is need to link across ECEC and school settings, there is often the need to link within settings around the needs of particular children.

How coherent are children's ECEC experiences?

In order to better understand current transition issues it is essential to look at children's early childhood experiences – the types of policies and provision for children – *before* primary education begins. The number and nature of children's transitions in their early childhood is linked, in part, to the structure, quality, and coherence of ECEC services in the country concerned. In some countries – including Belgium, the Czech Republic, Italy, the Netherlands and Portugal – policies and provision for children under compulsory school age are divided into education and welfare systems. This division generally follows the age of the child, with publicly-funded arrangements for children over three (or four) based in education departments; these services are usually open during the school day and are usually free. In these countries, the welfare services tend to be far less developed in terms of coverage, and usually require a parental contribution. Often the two systems of services differ in terms of staffing, funding, and programme orientation as well. These differences may create inequalities and lack of coherence for children and families (European Commission Childcare Network, 1996). In other countries – such as Denmark, Finland, Norway, Spain and Sweden – services for children under compulsory school age are part of a coherent system of ECEC provision, with unified national administration, and consistent staffing, funding and regulatory regimes. Services also tend to be open the full-day, eliminating the need for any 'wrap-around' provision.

Even within settings, coherence for children may vary, depending on how services are organised. In the first pattern, children are grouped according to age, often called the 'school model.' The second pattern is called the 'family model' because children of different ages are placed in the same group. ECEC in Greece, Spain, France, Ireland, UK (England and Wales) and the US tend to follow the school model of same-age grouping (at least for older children), while in Denmark, Germany, Finland, Norway and Sweden, the family model is more common. Some countries – such as Belgium, Italy, the Netherlands and Portugal – may adopt either model (European Commission, 2000). The age-integrated approach means that children may be part of the same group of several years before beginning school, and may give children and parents opportunities to establish important relationships with professionals and other children over time. The 'school model', however, leads to more frequent transitions, but anticipates the organisation that children will experience in most primary schools. In some countries, including Italy, Germany and Portugal, pre-schools and schools try to increase the continuity of children's educational experiences by encouraging teachers to move with their students to the next class or group for two or more consecutive years. This approach is known as 'looping' (Burke, 1997).

While coherent early childhood experiences are more likely to facilitate children's transitions from one sphere of life to another, and provide more continuity in their early learning and development, there is no guarantee that the relationship between these services and the compulsory school system will be coherent (EC Childcare Network, 1996).

When does the transition to primary school take place?

School starting age influences the timing and nature of children's transitions. First, it is important to look at what age children are *required* to attend primary school in different countries. While the starting age for compulsory primary education varies from four (Northern Ireland) to seven (Denmark, Finland and Sweden), children in most OECD countries make the transition to compulsory education at the age of six. In some countries, particularly those with less-developed ECEC provision, children may *typically* begin primary school prior to reaching compulsory school age. In the Netherlands and Great Britain statutory school age is five, but it is common practice for almost all young children to enrol in primary school on a voluntary basis at age four.[2] In Australia, Canada, New Zealand and the US primary schools commonly provide for children under six in pre-school or (pre-) kindergarten classes.

There is currently some debate concerning the appropriate age for children to start primary school. In Great Britain, there has been some concern about the suitability of learning environments for four-year-olds in reception classes where staff–child ratios may reach 1:30. In Italy and Portugal, lowering the compulsory school age to five has been discussed, and later rejected, as a means of providing equal educational opportunities for socially disadvantaged children, especially ethnic minority groups (Oberhuemer and Ulich, 1997). Lowering the age of school start is also a strategy to provide more places for younger children in ECEC. In Norway, when the six-year-olds began attending the free public schools, the supply of ECEC for children under six increased by 20,000 places. However, in countries that have adopted market approaches to ECEC (e.g. the UK and US), there is concern that as three- and four-year-olds move into free public education, the unit cost of provision for infants and toddlers will increase and consequently restrict access.

The most widespread criteria used to determine *access* to compulsory school is the age of the child. In only a few OECD countries is the child's maturity an additional criterion taken into account for admission to compulsory primary school, often for children who are under statutory school age. Maturity is assessed in various ways (e.g. medical or psychological examinations, aptitude tests, opinions of the educational team, future teachers, parents, etc.). Some countries specify the skills that children should master before starting compulsory school. Continuous assessment, particularly observation, is the most common approach adopted to monitor children's progress before entry to primary school. In parts of Belgium, France, Portugal and the UK, teachers also must record their assessments. In the UK (England and Wales), these skills are evaluated in the 'baseline assessment' at the beginning of primary school (European Commission, 2000).

Usually, school starting age must be reached during the calendar year in which the child starts school. In some countries, the required age must have been reached before a date which generally precedes or corresponds to the start of the school year. In Ireland, the Netherlands and the UK (England and Wales), children may start school during the school year, rather than at the beginning (e.g. first of the month or the term following the child's birthday) (European Commission, 2000). This practice of a rolling start, also common in Denmark and New Zealand, has been supported for pedagogical reasons as a means of making school start an individualised and personal event for the child, and for economic reasons, as a means of reducing the financial burden for municipalities (and parents) of having the child stay in the more expensive ECEC provision for a few extra months.

Although most children begin primary school at six, many are entering the school system much earlier. Most countries provide some form of non-compulsory school-based ECEC to provide a bridge to formal schooling. Pre-primary schools are the only form of ECEC provision for children from the age of two-and-a-half in Belgium and from the age of three in France and Italy, and nearly all children in these countries attend by age three. Many of these services are connected to, or co-located with, primary schools. In the Nordic countries, where a wide range of ECEC provision is available for children below compulsory school age (e.g. centre-based and family day care), children start school-based provision later, but there are moves toward the European norm of age six. In 1997, after 30 years of debate, Norway lowered its statutory school start from seven to six. Denmark and Sweden have kept compulsory school age at seven, but have introduced a free, voluntary pre-primary class in the primary schools for six-year-olds. In practice, therefore, almost all children enter the school system at age six. Since 2000, all six-year-olds in Finland, too, have a right to attend free pre-primary education, either in ECEC settings (e.g. day care centres) or in the primary schools.

What are the barriers to ensuring smooth transitions?

The obstacles to ensuring smooth transitions vary depending on the individual contexts and relationships that have developed among schools, families, and ECEC. However, information collected for the OECD project suggests that several main barriers to improved co-operation seem to be common across countries (Neuman, 2000). First, there may be *different visions and cultures* in ECEC and primary school. In many countries, ECEC and schools have developed independently of each other, without coherent or shared goals. Often, ECEC and primary school staff are trained in different pre-service and in-service training programmes, with varying content and orientation. As a result, ECEC and schools have adopted different objectives, pedagogical approaches and methods. Both professional groups may perceive increased co-operation as a threat to their different ways of working with children. The early childhood community has been concerned that more collaboration with the schools will lead to a downward pressure from the primary schools leading to a more narrow focus on literacy and numeracy. At the same time, many primary teachers are worried about the children who are not 'prepared' for formal schooling, and feel that pre-schools could benefit from a more educational focus. Not surprisingly, children may find it difficult to adjust to the new rules and routines, environment, teacher expectations and styles of interacting when they move from one culture to another (Shore, 1998).

Second, these philosophical differences are often reinforced by *structural divisions*. Not only is there often a break between services for children over and under three, but pre-school and primary programmes often fall under different administrative auspices, regulations, and inspection and monitoring regimes. These structural divisions may limit, or even prohibit, co-operation and collaboration. In addition, in most countries, teachers in compulsory education have enjoyed greater status and salaries than ECEC workers. Even within the early childhood workforce there may be disparities in training, pay and working conditions for staff depending on the setting and age of children served. These institutional barriers may make it challenging for professionals to form equal partnerships to support young children. Sometimes, it is difficult for ECEC programmes to establish links with schools because children may be assigned to many different 'feeder' schools in a wide geographical area. Yet, even when schools are located near ECEC settings (or even in the same building), structural and philosophical divisions may limit the opportunities for teachers and ECEC staff to discuss and share their goals and expectations concerning children's early learning and the important links between their respective institutions.

Third, *communication barriers* between staff and parents may weaken efforts to bridge children's learning from home to ECEC to school. Parents and teachers may hold different attitudes and beliefs concerning what their children should know and be able to do when they come to school, what they should experience in the first years of schooling, and what are the respective roles of teachers and parents in children's learning. Moreover, language, values, behavioural codes, and expectations may differ between children's homes or ECEC programmes and the school, making it difficult for children to adjust without efforts by both teachers and families to make them feel comfortable and supported. These different perspectives may remain buried without attention to ensuring open lines of communication. Since both teachers and parents play a large role in facilitating children's transitions, their disparate goals and attitudes may have far reaching effects on continuity in children's development and learning – especially when they begin primary school (Kagan and Neuman, 1997).

Strategies to improve children's transitions

Despite the challenges, many countries have explored and adopted strategies to promote coherence and continuity in the lives of young children. This section will discuss some of the approaches to smooth children's vertical and horizontal transitions in the following inter-connected areas: (1) structural continuity; (2) pedagogical and programme continuity; (3) professional continuity; and (4) continuity with the home. Under each area, several examples have been profiled in order to illustrate different approaches adopted in different countries.

Structural continuity

Driven by efforts to facilitate children's transitions, there has been a trend in initiatives to achieve more structural coherence across ECEC and compulsory education. In Belgium, the Czech Republic, Italy and Portugal, for example, the education system plays an important role in providing ECEC for children over three, and consistent regulations, funding and curricula have been developed across the education system. However, since policy and provision for children under three and out-of-school activities fall under different administrative auspices, there is still the risk of fragmentation. In Sweden, integrating responsibility for all forms of ECEC into the education system with compulsory schooling has led to an increasing public understanding that early childhood services combine care and learning – and represent a first and important phase of lifelong learning. There are signs that other countries, such as UK and Italy, may follow this model.[3]

In the context of decentralisation, regional and local governments may have more flexibility to experiment with integrating administration and policy development across age groups and sectors. In Australia, three states and territories – South Australia, Australian Capital Territory and Tasmania – have integrated children's services and education portfolios to facilitate structural continuity for young children. In Denmark, Italy, Norway, Sweden and the UK, an increasing number of local authorities have reorganised local administrations and political committees to bring together ECEC and schools (and sometimes other children's services), often within education departments. Some municipalities in Norway have integrated *barnehager* for children under six, leisure-time activities, schools *and* child welfare services into a 'Department for Growing Up,' with responsibility for a child's total environment; a few have brought together a range of other services such health, social security and eldercare under one department.

Administrative integration, however, is not the only way of creating coherence for children. At the national level, countries have adopted a range of innovative mechanisms to increase co-ordination for children and youth across different departments and sectors:

- In the French Community of Belgium, for example, the Minister for Childhood is responsible for both education (*école maternelle* and *primaire*) and children's services (infant-toddler and out-of-school). Although 'education' and 'care' services are still administratively divided, the appointment of a political leader with policy responsibility for all children under twelve favours co-ordinated policy development in the French Community.

- In Denmark, an Inter-Ministerial Committee on Children was set up in 1987 as an interdisciplinary body of fifteen Ministries with responsibility for matters relating to children and families. Chaired by the Ministry of Social Affairs, the main objective of the committee is to create coherence in areas relating to children and families and to promote cross-sector initiatives to improve the living conditions for children and young persons.
- Several governments have established an Ombudsman for Children as an autonomous institution that works across many different disciplines and areas of responsibility to promote children's rights and well-being, particularly through the implementation of the UN Convention on the Rights of the Child (Hodgkin and Newell, 1996).

Finally, many countries have recognised the importance of integrating education, social welfare, and health services in order to meet the wide-ranging needs of children and families, particularly those at-risk, in a holistic manner. Close co-operation among ECEC, school, and allied services, can help promote continuity in children's development and learning. These multi-agency initiatives sometimes target individual children and families, but more often they serve an entire community identified in need of special support:

- In the US, *Head Start,* is a federally-funded, community-based early inter-vention initiative, which provides comprehensive education, developmental, mental health, nutrition, and social services to poor families with young children. The programme includes an intensive parent and community involve-ment component. While Head Start has traditionally co-ordinated with the health, social, and mental health fields, increasingly, programmes are linking with child care services to provide full-day, year-round coverage for children of working parents.
- The UK recently introduced the interdepartmental anti-poverty initiatives *Sure Start* and *Sure Start Scotland*, which draw on the Head Start model, but are area-based, and include all children under four, regardless of family income. Sure Start uses a partnership approach to local service delivery which includes public, private, and voluntary sectors, community organisations and parents. In England, government-supported models of exemplary practice, *Early Excellence Centres,* offer a range of integrated services, including early years education for three- and four-year olds, full-day care for children birth to three years, drop-in facilities, outreach, family support, health care, adult education, and practitioner training.
- In Belgium (Flemish and French Communities), the Netherlands, Portugal and the UK, *educational priority policies* allocate extra resources to pre-schools

and schools located in designated socially, culturally, and economically disadvantaged zones in order to improve the quality of children's educational experiences through a collaborative and multi-service approach. By targeting geographical areas, these programmes promote equal educational opportunities without stigmatising individual children.

Such linkages across services can help to promote interdisciplinary ways of working, minimise duplication of services, facilitate children's transitions, and assist parents in navigating available services. In particular, consolidating adminis-tration under education auspices provides an opportunity to strengthen the articulation between ECEC and school and to develop a coherent framework for regulation, funding, training and service delivery. However, there are concerns that as ECEC provision becomes more integrated with compulsory schooling, it will become more isolated from child welfare, health, and allied sectors, which points to the importance of integrating services at the local level. Specialists in some countries (e.g. Belgium, Denmark, England) also fear that the dominant culture of the school system has eroded some of the specific pedagogical methods of ECEC – particularly the emphasis on children's creativity and self-initiative – in favour of more formal teaching approaches. This has not been the experience in Sweden where ECEC has been recognised as a distinct stage of education, with its separate curriculum framework and staff with specialised training. Finally, making early childhood an important part of the educational system suggests that these services should be accessible to all children, like public schooling.

Pedagogical and programme continuity

Ensuring pedagogical and programme continuity from ECEC to primary school is another strategy to ease children's transitions. Most European countries have developed national curricula or frameworks for ECEC, which state the general objectives and specific aims of services for children in such areas as written and oral language, mathematics, art, science and physical education (European Commission, 2000). All of these documents make at least some reference to the importance of facilitating children's transitions and the need for co-operation and collaboration between ECEC and schools. Some countries have developed stronger conceptual links across age groups and settings, with particular attention to promoting continuity in children's learning during the important transition from ECEC to primary school:

• The French Community of Belgium has organised early schooling around three 'cycles of learning,' the first two covering the age groups from two-and-a-half to five and from five to seven. These cycles reinforce the structural and pedagogical links between pre-school and primary education, and enable the staff team to better adapt their methods to the rhythm and progress of each child. A primary goal is to assure that all children have access to the *socles de compétences* (basic competencies) necessary for their social integration and educational success. Developmental goals as well as competency goals related to numeracy, scientific enquiry and language are integrated into the curriculum.

- In Australia, a number of states and territories are developing curricular strategies to improve children's transitions. As an example, the new South Australian Curriculum Standards and Accountability (SACSA) Framework covers children from birth to eighteen across diverse school and non-school settings. With regard to children in the early years, the framework is divided into age ranges of birth to three, three to five, and five to eight. The goal is to build a seamless system of curriculum and services for young children. Transitions and continuity are key themes throughout the SACSA Framework.

- Sweden has developed three curricula for pre-school, compulsory school, and upper-secondary school that are linked conceptually by a coherent view of knowledge, development and learning. The goal is to promote an educational continuum for the first twenty years of lifelong learning, guided by the same fundamental values: democracy, the inviolability of human life, individual freedom and integrity, the equal value of all people, gender equality, solidarity with the weak and vulnerable, and respect for the environment. Both the pre-school and compulsory school curricula include guidelines that require staff at the pre-school through upper secondary levels to co-operate and to accord particular attention to children in need of special support during periods of transition.

These different curricular approaches can help improve the conceptual and pedagogical links between ECEC and schools, and promote increased continuity for children over the years. There is some concern about the dangers of a downward push from formal schooling when early childhood frameworks are linked with curricula for older age groups. On the other hand, as staff working with children in ECEC and primary schools in OECD countries increasingly collaborate around curricular issues, with much attention to children's transitions, they may develop new ways of understanding children's learning across a wide age span. This process can contribute to a synergy of cultures between schools and early childhood settings.

Professional continuity

Staff are key to ensuring coherence in the lives of children. Structural integration and curriculum guidelines may promote continuity and coherence in pedagogical work in ECEC and schools, but successful implementation depends greatly on the professionals who work with young children. Communication and collaboration between pre-school and school teachers can help ensure compatible programme philosophies, and broaden staff understanding of children's prior experiences and those that are likely to follow. Joint pre-service and in-service training may encourage staff to develop a core of common knowledge upon which to build partnerships. In several countries, teams of staff, with different training, have developed new ways of working together to overcome professional boundaries and promote coherence in children's lives:

- In Norway, when compulsory school age was lowered from seven to six in 1997, the government decided that the first four grades of primary school were to be based on bringing together the traditions of both the *barnehager* (kindergarten) and school to ease children's transition from one institution to the other. Both school teachers and *barnehage* teachers work with the six-year-olds in the new Grade 1, and early childhood staff can qualify to work in Grades 2 to 4 by completing an additional year of training. This process of change has provoked the rethinking of the relationship between the *barnehage* and the school, and their respective pedagogical methods. In practice, for example, this has led to more emphasis on learning through play, age-mixed activities, and organisation around themes (rather than subjects) in the early years of primary schooling.
- A similar initiative in Denmark is the 'co-ordinated school start'. Since 1989, local schools in Denmark, in co-operation with parents, may choose for children and staff in the pre-school class through Grade 2 of primary school to work closely together. Often the same pedagogues work with children during the school day and in leisure-time activities. This promotes continuity in children's relationships with adults and also facilitates opportunities for informal communication between staff and parents (Vilien, 1993). More recently, for pedagogical and economic reasons, the government has sought to strengthen co-operation between schools and centres for children under six by sponsoring local projects and activities involving *pedagogues* and teachers.
- In Portugal, about thirty-five *escolas básicas integradas* (integrated basic schools) were created to enable all children to stay in the same school environment from pre-school to completion of compulsory education. Pre-school classes for three- to six-year-olds are staffed by early childhood specialists, who have the same level of training, qualification and professional status as other teachers, but are trained separately. They are considered as equal members of the school staff and often participate in in-service training with their colleagues from other levels of the school system. Whenever possible, children are followed by the same group of teachers within the compulsory school system in order to strengthen relationships between the staff, the families and children. This approach seeks to provide coherent learning conditions for children and to enable improved management of educational resources.
- To encourage collaboration between early childhood staff and primary school teachers, in Sweden, there is a reform under way to partially integrate the training of different professionals. The new study programme would consist of joint training so that students who will work in pre-school, compulsory school, and upper secondary school obtain a common core of knowledge in areas such as teaching, special needs education, child and youth development, and interdisciplinary subjects. The remaining training would include

specialised studies and supervised field placement. Teachers in pre-school, the first years of compulsory school, and out-of-school provision would have the same qualification, but different specialisations, strengthening opportunities for teamwork and building closer links across different phases of lifelong learning.

Working in interdisciplinary teams across age groups and settings is a way to bridge children's experiences from ECEC to primary school. This approach gives children the opportunity to become more accustomed to the routines and styles of working in the primary years, while retaining some of the familiar aspects and traditions of the ECEC settings. Mixed-aged grouping in the early primary years – common ECEC practice in some countries – allows children to learn from each other and reduces same-age peer comparisons that can make children feel inadequate (Katz *et al.*, 1990). Similarly, by creating an extended family, looping can have positive effects on both children's learning and parental involvement (Burke, 1997). However, it is important that different workers are respected as equal members of the team, bringing different, but equally valuable, skills, knowledge and experiences to work with young children. Such teamwork, reinforced by joint in-service training, can provide an opportunity for staff from different fields to learn from others and reflect on their own practice.

Continuity with the home

A critical component of quality early childhood and primary settings is meaningful parent involvement. Continuity for children can be further strengthened when the engagement and support of families are nurtured over the years. In most countries, both ECEC provision and schools stress the importance of co-operation with the family, especially in periods of transition or difficulty. With the increasing heterogeneity of today's families, it is crucial for ECEC and schools to elicit and take into account parents' preferences and to adopt strategies that value ethnic, cultural, linguistic and other forms of diversity (Shore, 1998). It is also important for staff to create avenues for information sharing and open discussion with parents so that different understandings do not become a barrier to supporting children's transitions:

- Many Italian labour laws, as well as regional and local policies, now mandate parental leave to assist children and families during the delicate transition (*l'inserimento*) from home to ECEC setting. Diverse interpretations range from inviting parents to accompany the child during his or her initial transition into early childhood provision to having parents stay with their child in the centre for as long as it takes for both to feel at ease in the new setting.
- Similarly, in Sweden, when children begin pre-school, there is a two-week adjustment period when parents spend time with their children in the centre, which not only eases the transition for the child, but helps establish a positive

relationship between the parent and the ECEC setting. Such informal opportunities for parents to take part in ECEC and schools, and support their children's transitions can be encouraged by flexible working hours and arrangements that exist in several other countries (e.g. Belgium, Denmark, Finland, the Netherlands and Norway).

In order to provide coherence with the home, it is important for staff to engage in discussions with parents around their children's development and learning. These interactions can provide a opportunity for parents and staff to make explicit their different perspectives and work out any misunderstandings (Kagan and Neuman, 1997). These conversations may occur very informally when parents drop-off or pick-up their children. In addition, recorded observations and assessments of children can be a very valuable basis for more formal discussion between parents and staff about their children's early development and learning:

- Teachers in ECEC centres in Reggio Emilia, Italy use a form of continuous assessment and documentation to engage parents *and* the wider community in children's learning (Edwards *et al.*, 1993). Teachers record children's experiences in words, drawings, photos, and videos incorporating children's ideas, memories, and feelings, as well as teachers' observations of children's investigations and social interactions. Children have a compendium of images and words with which to explore understandings of the topics they have investigated. Teachers use documentation as a tool to research, reflect, and improve on their work with children. Documentation also offers parents and community members detailed information about what occurs in the pre-schools and provides opportunities for discussion of children's learning.
- Inspired by the Reggio approach, in Finland, child portfolios are part of ongoing quality improvement efforts. These portfolios of children's photos, drawings, and memories of significant moments, as well as teacher observations, are a record of each child's life and growth at the centre. Through the portfolio, programme aims are explained to parents with the objective of mobilising parental follow-up and of achieving a shared understanding of education. Children can take their portfolio with them when they change centres or start school, which may help smooth their transition from one setting to the other.
- Communication with parents is even more important to support children with special educational needs. In the US, under the Individuals with Disabilities Education Act (IDEA), parents have a legal right to be included in the development of a child's Individualized Education Plan (IEP) which lays out the educational goals and objectives for children from three to five years. Families of children from birth to two are required to have an Individualized Family Services Plan (IFSP) which is designed to build on each family's strengths, and provide the supports and required to ensure that each young child being served with special education services receives the appropriate supports and services.

Strategies to engage parents seek to help them support their children's development and learning in the home. They also may provide opportunities to identify any special educational needs. The process not only reinforces the important role of parents in their children's education, but also may give them the support to continue to be involved and engaged when children move from one early childhood setting to another or when they begin primary school. However, staff face many challenges to engaging parents, including, cultural, attitudinal, linguistic differences between parents and staff, and logistical barriers, such as transportation. When parents are working, it is often difficult for them to contribute to the life of the early childhood setting, especially if they are coping with other stresses. In all countries, barriers seem to particularly affect parents with modest educational levels or low socioeconomic backgrounds, those who are among the least empowered groups in society.

Conclusions

As a result of recent demographic, economic, and social developments, children are likely to experience many transitions of various forms in their young lives (Fthenakis, 1998), which present opportunities as well as challenges. A large proportion of children are growing up in lone-parent households, and many hail from linguistically, culturally and ethnically diverse families. In some cases, they are living through periods of poverty and deprivation. Perhaps the most significant change in modern childhoods is that increasingly, children are living a greater part of their early childhood in out-of-home settings, and often, in multiple settings with multiple caregivers. While transitions can be viewed as learning opportunities for children, there are risks that children who experience difficult transitions will have difficulties in adjusting to school, making friends, and face emotional and health problems (Kagan and Neuman, 1999). The early childhood field, with the support of national and local policies, has responded to these concerns.

Summary

This chapter has provided some examples to illustrate the range of approaches that have developed in different countries to address children's transitions across the spheres and periods of their lives. Strategies have focused on achieving structural, pedagogical, professional continuity, as well as developing strong ties with families. While further research on the implications of these different options is needed, some lessons for how to promote continuity and coherence emerge from this analysis. In particular, it seems important for countries to develop a systemic and integrated approach from birth through the early years of primary school. There is a need for countries to increase administrative integration and co-ordination, develop common goals and principles to guide practice, strengthen communication and collaboration across agencies and professionals, focus on training and ongoing professional development, and develop meaningful partnerships with families. In conclusion, while the existing structural and attitudinal barriers are formidable, countries have developed promising initiatives meriting further study and analysis.

Notes

1 The OECD reviewed twelve countries between 1998 and 2000: Australia, Belgium, the Czech Republic, Denmark, Finland, Italy, the Netherlands, Norway, Portugal, Sweden, the United Kingdom and the United States. Reports from the study are available at: http://www.oecd.org.
2 In the Netherlands the majority in parliament, with government support, recently agreed to lower compulsory school age to four years. New legislation is necessary before the policy will be put into place.
3 Two other OECD countries have fully integrated all responsibility for ECEC under education auspices: New Zealand in the late 1980s and Spain in 1990.

References

References to the factual information presented in this chapter may be found in OECD (2001), unless otherwise noted.

Burke, D.L. (1997) *Looping: Adding Time, Strengthening Relationships*. ERIC Digest. Champaign, IL: ERIC Clearinghouse on Elementary and Early Childhood Education.

Edwards, C., Gandini, L. and Forman G. (eds) (1993) *The hundred languages of childhood*. Norwood NJ: Ablex.

European Commission Childcare Network (1996) *A Review of Services for Young Children in the European Union 1990–1995*. Brussels: Author.

European Commission. DG Education and Culture (2000) *Key Data on Education in Europe 1999–2000*. Luxembourg: Office for Official Publications of the European Communities.

Fthenakis, W. (1998) 'Family transitions and quality in early childhood education', *European Early Childhood Education Research Journal* 6(1), 5–18.

Hodgkin, R. and Newell, P. (1996) *Effective Government Structures for Children: Report of a Gulbenkian Foundation Inquiry*. London: Gulbenkian Foundation.

Kagan, S.L. (1991) 'The strategic importance of linkages and the transition between early childhood programs and early elementary school'. *Sticking Together*. Summary of National Policy Forum. Washington, DC: US Department of Education.

Kagan, S.L. and Neuman, M.J. (1997) 'Defining and implementing school readiness: challenges for families, early care and education, and the schools'. In T.P. Gullotta, R.P. Weissberg, R.L. Hampton and G.R. Adams (eds), *Healthy Children 2010: Establishing Preventative Services* (pp. 61–96), Thousand Oaks, CA: Sage Publishers.

Kagan, S.L. and Neuman, M.J. (1999) 'Lessons from three decades of transition research', *The Elementary School Journal* 98(4), 365–80.

Katz, L., Evangelou, D. and Hartman, J.A. (1990) *The Case for Mixed Age Grouping in Early Education*. Washington, DC: National Association for the Education of Young Children.

Neuman, M.J. (2000) 'Hand in hand: Improving the links between ECEC and schools in OECD countries'. In S.B. Kamerman (ed.), *Early Childhood Education and Care: International Perspectives* (pp. 177–217). New York: The Institute for Child and Family Policy at Columbia University.

Oberhuemer, P. and Ulich, M. (1997) *Working with Young Children in Europe: Provision and Staff Training*. London: Paul Chapman Publishing.

OECD (2001) *Starting Strong: Early Childhood Education and Care*. Paris: Author.

Shore, R. (1998) *Ready Schools. A Report of the Goal 1 Ready Schools Resource Group*. Washington, DC: National Education Goals Panel.

Vilien, K. (1993) Provision for preschool children in Denmark. In T. David (ed.), *Educational Provision for Our Youngest Children: European Perspectives* (pp. 18–34). London: Paul Chapman.

Chapter 2

The importance of social adjustment for future success

Anna Kienig

Introduction: the Polish context

In Poland pre-school education is treated as the first level of the education system. The pre-school setting is an independent educational and teaching institution for children aged three to seven. When children are admitted to a pre-school setting at the age of three, most of them have not had any pre-school experience. The kindergarten admits children at the age of six and works for an average of five hours a day. Most pre-school settings are open for five to eleven hours a day. Teachers work shifts, caring for an average of twenty-three children in pre-schools and sixteen children in kindergarten.

The pre-school curriculum contains the basic aims, tasks and skills that are considered important to be developed in a pre-school child. The aim of pre-school settings is to provide families with day-care support, to help children with social and emotional development, to provide children with academic skills and to prepare them for school. The preparation consists of stimulating the child's general development and teaching basic mathematics and reading skills. The most important part of pre-school education is the child's development and meeting his/her needs.

A theoretical framework

Adjustment to the pre-school environment, understood as adaptation to non-familial situations, is a central experience for children in the early years (Levy-Shift, 1983). The process of socialisation in early childhood depends on adjustment to the pre-school setting, with adjustment to the new situation being seen as a critical outcome of successful transition (Margetts, 2000).

There are many theoretical concepts to describe transition to a new environment (Cowan, 1991; Fthenakis, 1998; Fabian, 1998). The theoretical framework for this chapter is based on Bronfenbrenner's (1979) theory where adjustment to the institution outside the family is defined as an ecological transition, which means changes in identity, roles and relations. 'An ecological transition occurs whenever a person's position in the ecological environment is altered as the result of a change in role, setting, or both' (Bronfenbrenner, 1979, definition 6, p.26).

Adjustment to the pre-school setting is the first ecological transition between two microsystems or two educational environments: the family setting (primary developmental context) and the pre-school setting (secondary developmental context). The process of adjustment requires meeting the demands of these two environments. The academic and social goals of the pre-school environment are different from those of home (Rimm-Kaufman and Pianta, 1999). The differences between the requirements set by these two settings may invite problems related to pre-school adjustment. This requires a flexible approach on the part of the child and the modification of earlier learned habits.

Analysis of the children's first contacts with an institutional setting reveal that they are often of a negative character and are connected with stress and strong emotional experiences of both the child and his mother (Wall, 1986; Kontopoulou, 1997; Griebel and Niesel 1997, 1999; Burtscher, 1997). A child is disorientated during the first days in the pre-school setting and does not know who he should establish an emotional relationship with and who will satisfy his needs. A child emotionally attached to his mother, who has been fulfilling his vital needs, when left on his own in a strange setting experiences a generalised anxiety, because he has lost physical contact with the object of his attachment and lacks control over anything that may happen in the pre-school (Kondo-Ikemura, 1999). This condition deprives the child of a sense of security and the emotional strain it causes, disorganises cognitive activities, reduces his motor abilities and does not favour the operation of orientation and exploration reflexes. This influences negatively the adjustment processes to a new environment. The condition of prolonged stress results in strong negative emotions such as anxiety, fear, concern, irritation, anger and rage (Cowan, 1991; Griebel and Niesel, 1999). Lack of a sense of safety in children causes severe emotional reactions (Lubowiecka, 2000). The stress results in various alterations of behaviour.

The beginning of pre-school education is a time when many worrying examples of children's behaviour can be observed (Kienig 1999a; 2001). A poor adjustment to pre-school education may result in behavioural problems and even disharmonies of the children's development (Kienig, 1998, 1999a). On the other hand, a harmonious course of pre-school adjustment results in the child's ability to satisfy his own needs within the environment and to stand up to its requirements. The pre-school setting defines certain requirements for children when they are admitted for the first time. The most important are the child's social abilities such as establishing social relations with other children and adults (Taylor, 1991; Sameroff and McDonough, 1994; Dunlop, 2000) or co-operative behaviour while playing. The way children react to staying at the pre-school centre and whether or not they are eager to join the group and separate from their parents is also an important indicator. Organisation of the activities in a pre-school setting entails certain 'self-care' abilities of the child (such as eating, getting dressed and undressed, going to the toilet).

According to Bronfenbrenner (1979), Hartup (1979, 1980), Wall (1986) and Wolchik, Sandler and Braver (1987) the positive effects of the first contact with a new environment are conditioned by whether or not the child is emotionally supported in this period. The first contact with a new setting such as the pre-school setting is helped if it is made in the company of at least one person (for example, the mother) who has previous experience of a similar situation. Wall (1986) emphasised that the strain that accompanies the child's adjustment to a new situation may be so strong that it may disrupt normal routines and cause unusual behaviour (for example, a recurrence of bed-wetting). It is due to the adults' conduct whether this disruption of normal behaviour will be of a passing nature or will cause long-term developmental disturbances. Repeated situations of where the child is faced with tasks beyond their capabilities and a simultaneous lack of help from adults may even result in the child's development regressing, and cause the feeling of sadness in many children, especially during the initial period in a pre-school group. Therefore the role of the family is crucial, and they should see to it that the tasks the child faces are compatible with his capabilities, so that he can match them positively. It is best if the family supports the child in their adjustment to new situations and prepares him/her for entry into the new setting (Domitrovich and Bierman 1999; Griebel and Niesel, 1999, 2000; Kienig, 1999b; Dunlop, 2000). Fabian (2000) suggests that '... families can help children to develop strategies for approaching new situations, coping with change and solving problems before they start school'.

The adjustment process is extremely complex and relations between early adaptive processes and behaviour problems in later social development are varied and not always direct (Sroufe and Rutter, 1984). It is supposed that early maladjustment to the pre-school setting might create serious problems in the further social adjustment of children to other settings (Ladd and Price, 1987; Taylor, 1991; Le Mare, 1999). Adjustment to the pre-school setting forms a pattern for further ecological transitions, influences the ability of the child to function in different environments and, moreover, the consequences of the early adjustment process have a long-term influence on behaviour in the ensuing transitions from one environment to another (for example, from kindergarten to school).

Method

This study, exploring transitions to different settings: pre-school, kindergarten and school, was conducted during a period of two years. In the first stage the study comprised thirty children aged 3.0–4.0 (from pre-schools) and thirty children aged 6.0–7.0 (from kindergarten). The data included a comparison of their adjustment process to the new setting by these two groups of children. In the second stage (one year later) the sample included thirty children aged 7.0–8.0 (the older children from the first stage). In this case the children's behaviour was compared during the transition process to the next new environment – from kindergarten to school.

The data included results of observations (children's activities and interactions with peers and teachers) and interviews with parents and pre-school teachers. The children from both groups were tested in the first month of their first school year in pre-school and at the end of this school year.

The process of adjustment was assessed by carrying out observations in each family and pre-school setting. Information about the conditions of the family and the child's development pattern was obtained from the parents and pre-school teachers using a questionnaire and a structured interview.

At the beginning of the school year the children's behaviour was assessed according to the following criteria:

- behaviour with regard of basic physiological needs
- emotional reactions
- social relationships with children of the same age and adults in the pre-school setting
- self-care skills
- play activities

A good adjustment to the pre-school setting was indicated by a lack of disruptions in any of these categories.

At the end of the school year, teachers assessed the social adjustment level of children with the aid of Schaefer and Aaronson's Classroom Behaviour Inventory Pre-school to Primary Scale (CBI). Additionally the six-year-old children were tested one year later, when they finished their first class in primary school.

Results

Stage one: transition to pre-school setting and to kindergarten

The analysis of adjustment to pre-school settings showed that most children had problems of different kinds and different degrees of adjustment to the new environment, which was shown in the types of behaviour problems. The following types of behavioural problems were found at the beginning of the pre-school year:

- disturbances in basic physiological needs (eating problems, sleep problems, enuresis)
- inappropriate emotional reactions (anger and aggression or withdrawal and low mood)
- disturbances in social relationships (inattentiveness, clinging behaviour)
- disturbances in self-care skills (refusal to engage in self-care)
- disturbances in play activities (destructive behaviour regarding toys, aggressive play) (see Figure 2.1).

All types of behavioural problems were found more frequently in the group of three-year-old children (77 per cent) than in six-year-old children (50 per cent).

The most frequently in three-year-old children were disturbances in play activity (77 per cent), self-care skills (47 per cent) and in social relationships (37 per cent). In six-year-old children most frequent were problems in play activity (43 per cent) and social relationships (30 per cent).

At the end of the school year (measured with CBI) three levels of adjustment were found:

- good adjustment
- minor problems of adjustment
- serious problems of adjustment (see Figure 2.2).

Adjustment problems were found more frequently again in the group of three-year-old children (54 per cent) than in six-year-old children (17 per cent). Three-year-old children presented almost the same level of minor adjustment problems, for example in the beginning of the pre-school year (37 per cent) but we observed fewer children with serious problems of adjustment (17 per cent).

Serious changes of adjustment level in six-year-old children were observed. Almost all of them achieved good levels of adjustment (83 per cent), only 7 per cent had minor problems of adjustment and serious adjustment problems were determined in the same 10 per cent of children. These results show that behaviour problems disturbing the course of adjustment have a lower tendency during the

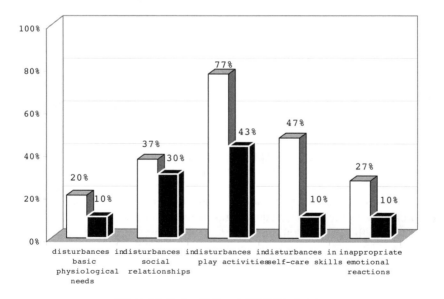

Figure 2.1 Types of behaviour problems at the beginning of the pre-school year

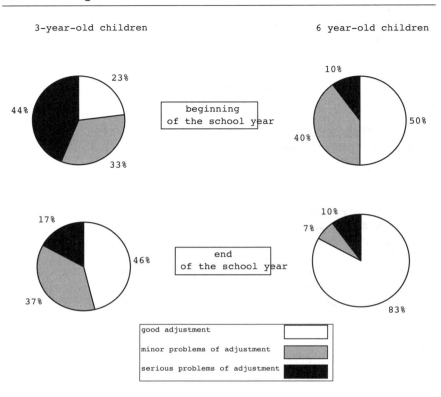

Figure 2.2 The level of adjustment (CBI values) of three-year-old and six-year-old
children

school year. The reason for this may be maturation of the nervous system and the
acquisition of emotional resilience or the acquisition of adaptive skills (for example,
the strategy of social behaviour) by the children. At the same time, the remaining
children (especially younger children) confirmed the rule, that if at the beginning
of the school year they presented behavioural problems, then they had a tendency
to such problems throughout the year more than children who had no disturbances
of this kind.

The data obtained confirm the assumption that there are clear relations between
the problems manifested in certain spheres of behaviour and pre-school adjustment
measured with CBI. When children entering a new setting present behaviour
problems, they also have both minor and serious problems of adjustment at the
end of the pre-school year (see Table 2.1).

The effect of behaviour problems during the first month in a pre-school setting
on the level of adjustment at the end of the school year was statistically significant
(r_{pbi} = point biserial correlation; p = significance level) (r_{pbi} = 0.58 for three-year-
old children, r_{pbi} = 0.53 for six-year-old children, $p < 0.001$). In the group of three-
year-old children the strongest correlation was found between the level of

Table 2.1 The effect of behavioural problems at the beginning of the pre-school year on the level of adjustment (CBI values) in the end of the pre-school year (%)

Level of adjustment (CBI values)	Adjustment without problems		Adjustment with problems	
	3-year-old children	*6-year-old children*	*3-year-old children*	*6-year-old children*
Good adjustment	23	50	23	33
Minor problems of adjustment	–	–	37	7
Serious problems of adjustment	–	–	17	10

adjustment and problems of play activities (r_{pbi} = 0.579, p < 0.001), self-care skills (r_{pbi} = 0.43, p < 0.001), social contact (r_{pbi} = 0.374, p < 0.05) and emotional reactions (r_{pbi} = 0.29, p < 0.001). In the group of six-year-old children, the strongest correlation was found between the level of adjustment and problems of social contact (r_{pbi} = 0.63, p < 0.001), play activities (r_{pbi} = 0.653, p < 0.001) and self-care skills (r_{pbi} = 0.462, p < 0.001).

These findings support the general hypothesis that three-year-old children have more problems adjusting to a new environment than six-year-old children.

Stage two: the effect of transition to kindergarten on transition to school

The results at this stage contain descriptions of the children's behaviour problems during the entry into two new settings: first into kindergarten and a year later to a primary school. Behavioural problems found during the process of adjustment to the new setting were (see Figure 2.3):

•   at the beginning of the pre-school year in 50 per cent of six-year-old children
•   at the end of the pre-school year in 17 per cent of six-year-old children
•   at the end of the first year in the primary school in 40 per cent of seven-year-old children.

At the end of the first school year (measured with CBI) three levels of adjustment were found (see Figure 2.4):

•   good adjustment
•   minor problems of adjustment
•   serious problems of adjustment.

At the end of first school year adjustment problems were found in 40 per cent of children. Ten per cent of them had minor adjustment problems and 30 per cent presented serious adjustment problems.

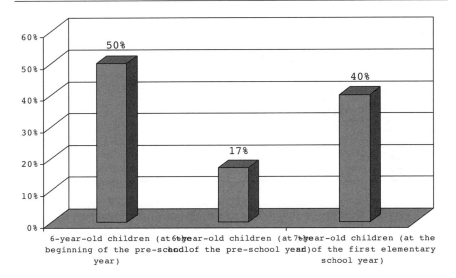

Figure 2.3 Dynamics of the adjustment process problems

The analysis of adjustment behaviour during the transition to a primary school showed that most children with adjustment problems at the beginning of the first pre-school year also had a tendency to behaviour problems in the first primary school year and these problems intensified.

Types of behaviour problems during transition to the new environment

The following types of behaviour problems were found in three-year-old children during transition to pre-school.

Problems in basic physiological needs

Problems of biological functioning manifested in three categories of behaviour connected with:

1   sleep
2   food intake
3   hygiene habits.

1   Sleep problems were observed both in a pre-school group (during noon rest) as well as at home. They were manifested by difficulty in falling asleep at appropriate times, night time anxiety and sleepwalking. This included problems during the course of sleep (light, restless sleep, frequent waking up).

6-year-old children (at the beginning of the pre-school year)

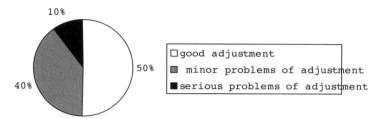

6-year-old children (at the end of the pre-school year)

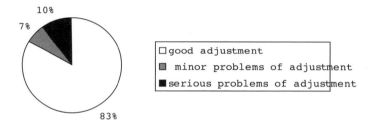

7-year-old children (at the end of the first elementary school year)

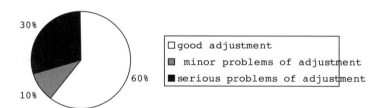

Figure 2.4 The level of adjustment (CBI values) of six-year-old and seven-year-old children

2   Inappropriate behaviour connected with eating habits was mainly manifested by refusal to eat at pre-school. Another behaviour (observed during meals at pre-school) was persistent vomiting before and during meals.

3   Problem behaviour connected with hygiene included unintentional wetting and relieving oneself at pre-school. Parents reported that these children had learnt to control the physiological needs before they joined the pre-school. Apart from the above problems, children had recurrent stomachache and persistent headaches.

Problems of basic biological functions were frequent and differentiated. Children most frequently presented problems connected with food intake, a little less frequently problems were connected with sleep. The least frequent were problems connected with hygiene. Most children had one symptom of basic biological functions problems, but some of them had more than two symptoms.

Problems of social contacts

Social problems were mostly observed at pre-school. They included avoiding contact or lack of distance in contacts with adults, avoiding contacts or conflict with other children.

The most frequently observed sign of social contact problems included avoiding contact with adults and other children. It took various forms, from watching other children and teachers from a distance to running away from them and hiding at pre-school.

In the case of some children, avoiding contact with other children was combined with the desire for close contact with adults. They were indifferent to other children, took no notice of them and chose adults (most frequently teachers) and stayed close to them all the time at pre-school (sitting on their laps, holding their hand or at least holding on to their clothing).

Avoiding contacts with adults and simultaneously coming into conflict with other children were also observed. These conflicts were mainly the result of taking toys away from other children or attempts to establish contact by other children. Aggressive behaviour towards other children was combined with a desire for continuous, direct contact with the teacher. Some children tried to stay on the teacher's lap all the time, and pushed away or pulled at other children who tried to get close to the teacher.

Children presenting social problems may be evidence of too rapid a transition from the family environment (where the number of persons to interact with is limited and the nature of these interactions are of a different nature) to a large pre-school group. This may exceed the developmental needs and capabilities of a three-year-old child, because it is difficult for the child to function in a social environment wider than the family.

Play activity problems

Play activities were evaluated on the basis of participation of children in play organised by the teacher, taking up spontaneous free play as well as the children's attitude to pre-school toys.

In all children, problems were mainly manifested by lack of interest in play activities organised by the teachers. They were reluctant to join the play, they only watched and tried to play separately from others, or were not interested at all in what was happening in the classroom. Interest in pre-school toys was observed in all children, even those who were not interested in play and played separately. Although they did not take the toys to play with, they took a close look at them from time to time.

Emotional reaction problems

Emotional problems were connected with negative reactions of the children to themselves or the pre-school. They included loud and prolonged crying during and after parting from their parents, fits of anger and aggression or feeling disheartened and reactions of fear observed at the pre-school. These kinds of behavioural problems were observed in some children throughout the whole time at pre-school, but they were most intensive during the so-called 'critical moments' of the routine, such as parents leaving, noon rest and meals.

Problems connected with anger and aggression were demonstrated by loud screaming, throwing themselves on the floor, stamping their feet, banging their heads and fists against the floor, pushing other children and the teacher away.

The children directed their aggressive behaviour either against themselves, for example banging their heads against the floor, pulling laces out of their shoes, or against objects in the classroom, for example, kicking furniture or throwing toys. More rarely their anger and aggression were directed towards other people, and then they were characterised by considerably less power and intensity and were manifested by pushing away other people or pulling themselves out of the teacher's hands.

The above problems were short-lived and they usually gave way after three or four days of the children's time at pre-school. In some children aggression and anger transformed into withdrawal or reactions associated with fear.

Problems connected with low mood and fright reactions were observed in some children. These children were weepy not only in the critical situations mentioned earlier, but all the time at pre-school. They also showed fear of strange people or rooms (for example, entering the pre-school bathroom). These kinds of problems were more frequent in boys than in girls. Problems connected with subdued and fearful reactions lasted longer. In some cases they were present for over a month.

It may be assumed that emotional problems indicated aversion and a negative emotional attitude to pre-school in most children beginning their pre-school education.

Self-care ability problems

The level of self-help ability was evaluated in situations connected with feeding, washing, getting undressed and getting dressed, and going to the toilet at pre-school.

The children being studied coped best with washing and satisfying their personal hygiene needs. Only one child needed the teacher's assistance in washing hands. The assistance of adults was also necessary in the case of children who had difficulties in satisfying their personal hygiene needs, such as using toilet paper and flushing the toilet.

Basic abilities connected with feeding, getting undressed and getting dressed were observed in most children, but only a few of them tried to do it by themselves.

Most of them expected assistance from the pre-school staff and with a little help or even encouragement from the adults they were coping with self-care. Many children made little attempt at feeding, getting dressed or undressed, despite encouragement from the adults, while the remainder did not even try to eat, get dressed or undressed unaided. These children, for a few days (from three to six) were attended by the pre-school staff, and only after this time made attempts at self-care activities.

In about a third of the children when they enter a new environment, activities connected with self-care were non-existent. These children started to use their abilities only after getting accustomed to the new environment, which usually took about a week.

The organisation of pre-schools in Poland (admitting all children to the first grade at the same time into several groups of children of the same age) does not make it easier for a child to cope with the requirements of pre-school. In the case of overcrowded groups, a pre-school setting, instead of stimulating and supporting the children's development in all aspects (as it is assumed in the policy of a pre-school) becomes the first hindrance on the way to harmonious development. There are no programmes involving educational activities adjusted to the stage of development, making it possible for the child actively to learn and create his/her own self.

Among the numerous factors conditioning the course of pre-school adjustment, the most crucial is a positive emotional attitude of the child to the pre-school, which is accompanied by the easy establishment of social relations both with children of the same age and adults, activity while playing, considerable independence and also a lack of problems of basic biological functions.

To summarise, the goal of this study was to answer the following questions:

* What kind and frequency of behavioural problems occur during adjustment to the new setting?
* How do transitions to various settings in early childhood change?
* Are there any connections between pre-school and school adjustment?

Conclusions

Some children during the entry to the pre-school environment are under enormous stress. Most of them had problems with adjustment to the new environment of various kinds and degrees, which manifested itself in the forms of behaviour problems. As Bronfenbrenner has suggested, adjustment to the pre-school setting forms a prototype for later ecological transitions, influences the ability of the child to function in different environments and the consequences of early adaptation process have a long-term influence. Most children with adjustment problems at the beginning of the first pre-school year also had a tendency to behaviour problems in the first elementary school year and these problems intensified. All these problems have an impact on the child's commitment to schooling and motivation for learning.

There is a growing need for direct, close contact between families and pre-school and school teachers. From the parents' perspective most children have many adjustment problems during the entry to pre-school, but only very few parents try to help their children in this transition.

It is necessary to develop special programmes to make the transition to pre-school less stressful for children and their families. Most Polish teachers believe the pre-school setting helps children in their adjustment to a new environment through exchange of information with parents about their child, his special needs and the family background. Parents can help prepare their children to entry into pre-school mainly by developing a positive attitude and giving emotional and social support during the transition.

Children's success in achieving a transition may also be facilitated by characteristics of the new setting. The pre-school teachers can help children in this first transition and adapt the pre-school setting to the biological and psychological needs and developmental abilities of the child, for example by providing opportunities for gradual entrance to the pre-school group, opportunities for getting to know the new environment and reducing the number of children in pre-school groups.

References

Bronfenbrenner, U. (1979) *The Ecology of Human Development: Experiments by Nature and Design.* Cambridge, MA, and London: Harvard University Press.

Burtscher, I.M.R. (1997) 'Pedagogical advice for parents and early childhood teachers to ease children's separation from their mother when starting nursery school – a critical analysis'. Paper presented at the 7th European Conference on the Quality of Early Childhood Education, Munich, September.

Cowan, P.A. (1991) 'Individual and family life transitions: a proposal for a new definition', in P.A. Cowan and M. Hetherington (eds), *Family Transitions: Advances in Family Research*, Vol. 2. Hillsdale, NJ: Lawrence Erlbaum.

Domitrovich, C.E. and Bierman, K.L. (1990) 'Parenting practices and child social adjustment: multiple pathways of influence'. Paper presented at the Biennial Meeting of the Society for Research in Child Development, Albuquerque.

Dunlop, A.W.A. (2000) 'Perspectives on the child as a learner: should educators' views of pre-school and primary children differ?'. Paper presented at the 10th European Conference on the Quality of Early Childhood Education, London.

Fabian, H. (1998) 'Developing a conceptual framework for children's induction to the reception class and their transitions through school'. Paper presented at the 8th European Conference on the Quality of Early Childhood Education, Santiago de Compostela.

Fabian, H. (2000) 'Empowering children for transitions'. Paper presented at the 10th European Conference on the Quality of Early Childhood Education, London.

Fthenakis, W.E. (1998) 'Family transitions and quality in early childhood education', *European Early Childhood Education Research Journal* 6(1), 5–17.

Griebel, W. and Niesel, R. (1997) 'From family to kindergarten: a common experience in a transition perspective'. Paper presented at the 7th European Conference on the Quality of Early Childhood Education, Munich.

Griebel, W. and Niesel, R. (1999) 'From kindergarten to school: a transition for the family'. Paper presented at the 9th European Conference on the Quality of Early Childhood Education, Helsinki.

Griebel, W. and Niesel, R. (2000) 'The children's voice in the complex transition into kindergarten and school'. Paper presented at the 10th European Conference on the Quality of Early Childhood Education, London.

Hartup, W.H. (1979) 'The social worlds of childhood', *American Psychologist* 34(10), 944–50.

Hartup, W.H. (1980) 'Peer relations and family relations: two social worlds', in M. Rutter (ed.), *Scientific Foundations of Developmental Psychiatry*. London: Heinemann Medical Books.

Kienig, A. (1998) 'Developmental disharmonies and adaptation of child to pre-school setting', *International Journal of Early Years Education* 6(2), 143–53.

Kienig, A. (1999a) 'Dysharmonie rozwojowe a adaptacja dzieci do przedszkola'. Unpublished doctoral thesis, University of Warsaw.

Kienig, A. (1999b) 'Adjustment to new setting in the early years: how to help children in this transition'. Paper presented at the 9th European Conference on Quality in Early Childhood Education, Helsinki.

Kienig, A. (2001) 'Przystosowanie dzieci trzyletnich do życia w grupie przedszkolnej', in S. Guz (ed.), *Wychowanie przedszkolne na przełomie tysiąclecia*. Warsaw: Wydawnictwo WSP TWP.

Kondo-Ikemura, K. (1999) 'Relations between separation responses from parents and their social adaptation in day-care centre in Japan'. Paper presented at the Biennial Meeting of the Society for Research in Child Development, Albuquerque.

Kontopoulou, M. (1997) 'Adjustment difficulties in pre-school education: the views of educators'. Paper presented at the 7th European Conference on the Quality of Early Childhood Education, Munich.

Ladd, G.W. and Price, J.M. (1987) 'Predicting children's social and school adjustment following the transition from pre-school to kindergarten', *Child Development* 58(5), 1168–89.

Le Mare, L. (1999) 'Temperament and socio-emotional adjustment in the early childhood classroom'. Paper presented at the Biennial Meeting of the Society for Research in Child Development, Albuquerque.

Levy-Shift, R. (1983) 'Adaptation and competence in early childhood: communally raised kibbutz children versus family raised children in the city', *Child Development* 54(6), 1606–14.

Lubowiecka, J. (2000) *Przystosowanie psychospoleczne dziecka do przedszkola*, Warszawa: WSiP.

Margetts, K. (2000) 'Transition to school – complexity and diversity'. Paper presented at the 10th European Conference on the Quality of Early Childhood Education, London.

Rimm-Kaufman, S.E. and Pianta, R.C. (1999) 'Patterns of family-school contact in pre-school and kindergarten', *School Psychology Review* 28(3), 426–38.

Sameroff, A. and McDonough, S.C. (1994) 'Educational implications of developmental transitions', *Phi Delta Kappan* 76(3), 188–93.

Sroufe, L. and Rutter, M. (1984) 'The domain of development psychopathology', *Child Development* 54, 173–89.

Taylor, A.R. (1991) 'Social competence and the early school transition', *Education and Urban Society* 24(1), 15–26.

Wall, W.D. (1986) *Twórcze wychowanie w okresie dzieciństwa*. Warszawa: PWN.

Wolchik, S., Sandler, I. and Braver, S. (1987) 'Social support: its assessment and relation to children's adjustment'. In N. Eisenberg (ed.), *Contemporary Topics in Developmental Psychology*. New York: John Wiley and Sons.

Chapter 3

From home to childcare centre
Challenges for mothers, teachers and children

Carmen Dalli

The trend to participate in early childhood services outside the home is fast becoming a story of our time, a narrative that more and more families and children have to tell as part of their life history; a story constructed in, and of, the world they inhabit.

This chapter explores the lived reality of the transition from home to the first group-based early childhood services as experienced by five under-three-year-old children, their mothers and at least one teacher in a children's childcare centre. It draws on a study conducted in five licensed childcare centres in a major city in Aotearoa, New Zealand. The study used a qualitative case study approach from which stories of the participants' experience of starting childcare were constructed.

The stories show that starting childcare was a complex experience that posed challenges for all involved.

Existing research on starting childcare

Research on the first transition from home to the early childhood setting has focused on how children have coped with entry into the childcare or pre-school setting. The focus of research has been on children; adults have participated as informants about the children's experiences rather than as participants in the experience in their own right.

Retrospective questions about parents' first use of childcare services have yielded reports of satisfaction with both the choice and the quality of the service (e.g. Barraclough and Smith, 1996; Bradbard and Endsley, 1980; McCartney and Phillips, 1988; Rolfe *et al.*, 1991; Shinn *et al.*, 1990). In New Zealand, Farquhar (1991) and Renwick (1989) noted that mothers typically see childcare as affecting their children more than themselves. McCartney and Phillips (1988) found that caregivers were central in mothers' reports of satisfaction and dissatisfaction with their childcare arrangements and Rolfe *et al.*'s study of Australian mothers of infants found that mothers experienced their adjustment to childcare as a process that was 'complex and diverse ... often disjointed ... and full of irresolvable dilemmas and emotional chaos' (p. 31).

Teachers' experiences of starting childcare are even less researched than parents' experiences. With few exceptions (Ayers, 1989; Johnston and Brennan, 1997), references to teachers' experiences appear mostly in practitioner-oriented writings offering good-practice suggestions (Bailey, 1992; Balaban, 1985; Daniel, 1998).

Psychoanalytic studies of starting childcare have focused on the issue of separation (e.g. Janis, 1964; Meltzer, 1984; Robbins, 1997). Meltzer suggested that the absence of the mother leads children to develop a substitute relationship with the teacher. He argued that entry into the group situation of an early childhood centre represented entry into a form of tribal culture for which the child needs to learn the rules using 'primitive social impulses' (p. 100) to meet other children's aggression.

From an attachment theory perspective, research has explored whether use of childcare has a detrimental effect on children's relationship with their mother (e.g. Ainslie and Anderson, 1984; Bretherton and Waters, 1985). A few studies have suggested that the nature of children's attachment relationship to their mother strongly influences the relationship they develop with their teachers (e.g. Petrie and Davidson, 1995).

Using notions from temperament theory, children's response to starting pre-school has been discussed in terms of 'adjustment' to both peers and centre adults, as well as to the new environment (e.g. Marcus *et al.*, 1972; Mobley and Pullis, 1991).

Taking a more social-psychological perspective, Blatchford *et al.* (1984) looked at entry into an early childhood setting as an experience of socialisation. In a study of three- to four-year olds in British nursery schools Blatchford *et al.* reported that after an initial period when the new children appeared to lack the necessary information about 'rules, rituals and power structure' (p. 157), children rapidly learned to participate in high levels of social interaction. Similarly Feldbaum *et al.* (1980) reported that within their first week of attending at a pre-school, the behaviour of the twelve three- to four-year olds in their study became more similar to that of the established group members.

A children's perspective approach to studying entry into early childhood settings is very recent and is illustrated in the work of Pramling and Lindahl (1991, 1994) in Sweden and Thyssen (2000) in Denmark.

The current study

My study used a qualitative case study approach that drew on phenomenological methods to explore how infants acted in the 'life-world' of the childcare setting. Qualitative observations using pen and paper and video-recordings of the children's interactions with the adults, their peers and the environment allowed access to the children's experiences of starting childcare. Interviews with the teachers and the parents, my own field notes, and journal records kept by the adults allowed me to explore the parents' and teachers' experiences alongside the children's.

The participants in my study were four girls and one boy aged between 15 to 26 months, five mothers and six teachers (see Table 3.1).

Narrative analysis of the data (Polkinghorne, 1995) revealed that while the separation issue was important for all the participants, there were many other themes that unfolded.

The mothers' stories: a multifaceted experience

Am I doing the right thing?

The mothers' lived reality of starting childcare emerged as one of complicated emotions. Helen, talking about her daughter Maddi reflected: 'It's been a bit hard in terms of feelings. Clearly, she'd prefer not to be left ... There's a bit of perseverance required'. Two months into starting childcare Helen wrote in her journal: 'I am having second thoughts about leaving Maddi. Perhaps she is still too young and I am pushing her to do something she isn't ready to do'.

Helen spoke about feeling 'guilty'. She weighed up these feelings against the benefits that she perceived that childcare would give her daughter:

> I felt guilty about wanting to leave Maddi ... The thing I feel guilty about is that I think I can give Maddi the best care but ... there are things she can do there that perhaps she wouldn't do at home.

Picking up viruses and infections was a worry for Jean. Helen echoed this in her statement that she was not sure she was happy that Maddi had gone outside in

Table 3.1 Names of participants, their relationship and type of centre in which case studies were conducted

Case	Child's name and age in months at start	Parent/s	Teacher/s	Type of centre
CS1	Nina, 16m	Jean	Sarah	Half-day community crèche; community hall venue, parent co-operative management
CS2	Maddi, 15m	Helen	Anna and Sam	Sessional community crèche; community hall venue, parent co-operative management
CS3	Shirley, 17m	Deborah	Joan	Half-day; parent co-operative management
CS4	Julie, 18m	Lyn	Patti	Full-day; incorporated society
CS5	Robert, 26m	Paula and Michael	Lorraine	Full-day; age-segregated privately-owned

the middle of winter without wearing a jacket and hat. Implicated in Helen's concern about her daughter's health and safety was the suggestion that her control over her daughter's well-being was under threat.

The mothers also needed reassurance about what happened to their children when they were not present. A feeling of needing to 'keep on side with the teacher' was evident in comments such as Lyn's: 'I don't want to be seen to be criticising'. These highlighted the vulnerability of the mothers in trusting their child to adults whom they did not know, and could not personally monitor.

Developing trust in the teacher

Developing trust in the teachers was central in the mothers' accounts of their relationships with the centre teachers. The mothers identified strategies that made them feel supported and listened to including regular feedback from the teachers and information sharing; respect for the way they liked to do things with their child; being able to ring the centre to check how their child was doing; and having guidance on how they might help ease the separation (e.g. taking a familiar object from home). The mothers also noticed how 'tuned in' the teacher was to their child and whether they felt reassured about the teachers' competence by the way the teacher responded to their child. Jean's journal entries illustrate this:

> I thought Sarah was very good. She seems to be a thoughtful person, prepared to give Nina the time she requires over this settling-in phase. She has supported my decision to take the settling-in period slowly. I find her reassuring...
>
> When Nina suddenly became very distressed ... I wondered if I was doing the right thing ... if Sarah hadn't been as positive as she was, I would have said: 'is it worth it?'. But because Sarah was so calmly reassuring, it settled it.

In Nina's case study and Shirley's, a steady growth emerged in the trust between mother and teacher. In the other three case studies, however, the absence of substantive feedback, or information, and structural issues such not having one teacher to regularly speak to about one's child, or the perception that there were not enough adults for the number of children, were experienced as unhelpful by the mothers.

Working out the rules of the game

The mothers were aware that the centres had implicit rules and routines that they needed to discover. Helen said that she had expected the staff to 'give [her] an idea of the rules in place for my child' and Jean explained that while in the centre, she 'tried to pick up on a few things and fit in'. The mothers would have preferred guidance on the teachers' expectations. Lyn said: 'I have no idea what they [the teachers] saw my role there as. I find I have to ask them specific questions to find out things – they don't volunteer a lot of information'.

Being there for the child

One aspect of their role that the mothers were all very clear about was their role in relation to their child. They saw this as providing 'security' and 'support' in a situation of transition. Lyn explained that her presence during the orientation visits was as 'a comforter to Julie if she felt insecure' and 'to make Julie feel that she wasn't just being dumped there – to keep reassuring her that it was alright for her to be there'.

The mothers' narratives clearly indicated that for them, starting childcare was a multifaceted experience. They experienced deep emotions where positive feelings about the potential benefits to their child had to be balanced against the less desirable feelings of apprehension, guilt and general ambivalence about whether they were doing the right thing. Evidence that the teacher was 'tuned in' to their child was reassuring to the mothers as they sought to work out their new role of mothers using childcare.

The teachers' stories: theories of practice about starting childcare

As I explored the teachers' accounts of how they settled-in the case study children, it became clear that each teacher had a *theory of practice* about how best to handle this event (Dalli, 2000). Each theory of practice contained a key phrase, or a central image, which appeared to capture the understanding individual teachers had about the nature of the settling-in event. In each 'theory' it was possible to define a number of principles that teachers felt were important together with specific practices that they advocated. The theories of practice also seemed closely aligned to the policies of the childcare centres. The analysis of the data showed that the teachers' practices made a difference to the quality of the children's experiences. Nina's and Maddi's experiences illustrate this.

Nina and Maddi started childcare in two different centres with different policies and different theories of practice.

Nina's case study: 'weaning them in'

Nina went into a centre where she was immediately allocated Sarah as her primary caregiver. Sarah's theory of practice was captured by her phrase that settling-in was about 'weaning them in'. Sarah explained that it was 'better for a child to develop a deep relationship with one adult than a superficial relationship with four adults. When they are comfortable with one person, then they'll branch out'.

In Sarah's theory of practice, the mechanism through which a deep relationship could develop was 'focused treatment' from one adult. This would 'wean them in' to the centre and make them settle quicker than if they were 'dropped into it' or 'just dumped'. True to these principles, from the moment that Nina stepped into the centre, Sarah's behaviour became that of providing focused treatment: she initiated approaches to Nina, accepted Nina's towards her and remained consistently attentive to Nina's cues. At times Sarah used Nina's focus of attention to introduce her to some of the centre's rules (e.g. wearing an apron when painting; handwashing after painting), and to build up an easy and comfortable relationship with her. Sarah's journal chronicled how well her aim of establishing a deep relationship was going. Every little sign of increased acceptance of her by Nina was scrupulously recorded: when Nina first allowed Sarah to wipe her dirty hands; when Nina first sought Sarah out for comfort; Nina's first happy nappy-change at the childcare centre; and Nina's increased dependence on Sarah when Nina started staying at the centre without her mother. Then, as Nina began to attend regularly on her own, Sarah traced how Nina gradually had more contact with the other centre adults and truly 'branched out'. Through Sarah's enactment of her theory of practice, the action that was 'promoted' to Nina was more direct contact with Sarah, and this effectively 'canalised' (Valsiner, 1985; Valsiner and Hill, 1989) Nina into the deep relationship with her that Sarah felt was required for a successful settling-in.

Maddi's case study: 'go with the flow'

Maddi's case study provides a different example of how the teachers' practice made a difference. Maddi's centre had a 'go-with-the flow' policy on settling-in. No written policy on settling-in existed, but the teachers' journal records and interview accounts showed that their practice was based on the principles that: (i) each child is an individual; (ii) that each child has a right to form their own preferences for adults; and (iii) that the mother has a primary role in the child's life. These three principles formed the basis of the centre's practice to not pre-allocate primary caregivers, to take the approach of 'wait and see' what the child wants, and to allow the parent to take the lead in how to handle the settling-in time.

In Maddi's case what unfolded from this approach was a period of time early in the settling-in experience when both Maddi and her mother Helen felt somewhat lost and un-supported. The lack of clear procedures for how to handle the settling-in, apart from the principle of 'going with the child', meant that for a while, there was no clear adult who consistently focused on Maddi's settling-in experience. Anna, who had volunteered as the participating teacher, appeared to operate the centre's normal practice of letting things unfold in their own time. For Maddi, this resulted in a somewhat slow and 'bumpy' start to establishing relationships with the centre adults, and ambiguity about what generally was expected of her at the centre. Over time, what emerged for Maddi was a decided preference to be with Sam. This created a 'de facto' system of primary caregiving which Sam had not sought, but which both Anna and Sam supported once they recognised Maddi's preference. The teachers put this down to their belief in respecting the children's right to choose, adding: 'we also understand that children will form bonds ... with different adults ... you can't take it personally'.

The teachers' explanation of their practice acknowledged that respecting the right of the child to choose a preferred adult could create tension among colleagues. This highlights that part of their experience of having a new child at the centre included dealing with their own emotional responses to the child's attempts to establish a relationship with them.

For the teachers, the starting childcare experience was clearly one that engaged them in new relationships that developed in the context of their theory of practice and their centre's policy. Establishing new relationships was not always a straight-forward process. At times the teachers were required to act not only to implement their theory of practice but also to monitor their own emotional responses within the experience. Additionally it was clear that the teachers' actions made a difference to how children experienced their new relationships with the teachers. This under-lines the important role teachers have in determining the quality of the experiences that children have.

The children's stories: learning to fit in

The stories about how teachers enacted their theories of practice can be read as stories in which the children's experience was scaffolded by the adults in line with the adults' particular view of how children should relate to them. Thus, the stories of children relating to adults can be read as narratives about 'learning to fit in' with the teachers' expectations as these were articulated in their theories of practice (Dalli, 2000).

The theme of 'learning to fit in' emerged as a strong one in other aspects of the children's experiences, including in their interactions with peers, and in their interactions with their environment – both at the physical level and at the level of rules and routines. This section illustrates this theme using cameos from Robert's and Shirley's experiences.

Learning to fit in: rules in a group setting

During Robert's first session of sole attendance at his centre he was described by his teacher Lorraine as 'fitting in to how things worked well … he seems to know what he can and can't do to avoid other children getting upset'.

The following cameo sets provide an insight into how Robert came to know how things worked in his centre with a particular focus on rules about 'ownership' and sharing of centre toys.

Cameo sets 1 and 2 are from Robert's first and second orientation visits. In cameo set 1, the rules, or lessons that Robert might have drawn from his interactions could have been:

Rule 1: If I try and take an object from someone, they may/will take it back.
Rule 2: If others reclaim an object they originally had, I can do that too.

Cameo set 1: 'ownership' rules in a group setting

Time   Orientation visit 1 of 4

08.32   Robert is at the dough table sticking bits of twig and flowers into a lump of dough making a 'garden'. Nancy, on Robert's left, stands up from her chair and Robert pulls her chair over to him. Nancy reclaims her chair. Teacher makes no comment.

10.38   Robert and one of the teachers are standing in the dress-up corner. Nancy comes over holding a toy helicopter that Robert had played with earlier in the day. Robert reaches out to the helicopter and takes it from Nancy. Nancy tries to take it back but gets sidetracked to another toy and Robert goes towards mum with the helicopter. Teacher and mother make no comment.

In cameo set 2, the first rule about ownership may have become elaborated as:

Rule 1 (elaborated): The child who first lays claim on an object retains a higher claim on that object and the teacher will support them.

Additionally, Robert may have understood that:

Rule 3: When more than one of a given item is available, it is more acceptable to choose an unclaimed instance of the item from the alternatives.

Cameo set 2: elaborating 'ownership' rules

Time   Orientation visit 2 of 4

12.10   Robert is exploring a toy truck alongside three other children; looks over at a bigger truck that Hugo is playing with. Robert now pushes a toy pram – he goes over to the large truck that Hugo has just let go of.
        Hugo yells: 'My truck' in protest to reclaim it and teacher Pam says: 'Robert, do you want a truck too? Which one do you want?' Robert chooses another large truck and takes it over to where mum is sitting.

12.31   Robert moves towards a group of children sitting around teacher Pam who is reading a story. He spots the large truck that Hugo had played with earlier and sits on it to listen to the story.

12.33   Hugo walks over to the group, he goes up to Robert on the truck and Robert gets off the truck. Teacher gives Robert another large truck to sit on.

It is possible to argue that by 12.33 of the second orientation visit, Robert had already learnt to comply with Rule 1 because, on seeing Hugo approach, Robert easily moved off the large truck that Hugo had originally claimed.

Cameo set 3: testing out 'ownership' rules

Time   Orientation visit 3 of 4
11.50   Robert is at the puzzle table; he looks up at the noise of a rocking
         horse that Bill (15 months) is riding. Robert leaves his puzzle and
         goes over to Bill on his rocking horse. He watches Bill intently
         who keeps on rocking. Robert gets on the bouncing bug that is
         beside Bill's rocking horse; now he moves over to another rocking
         horse beside Bill's one and rocks this one from behind. Bill gets off
         his horse and Robert immediately gets on it. Bill doesn't like this
         and protests, pulling at the horse's ears. Robert says 'No, no' and
         sits tight and Bill moves away.

Time   Sole attendance: week 1 of 6
08.03   Robert goes over to the dough table and hijacks a chair away from
         another (younger) boy and sits on it.

Cameo set 3, however, suggests that while Robert may have understood Rule
1, this did not stop him challenging it. Robert may have understood that he could
sometimes get what he wanted. Additionally this understanding could have included
the component that getting what one wanted was easier if the other claimant was
younger, and/or in the absence of a teacher.

Robert's behaviour in these cameo sets show that within the first four weeks of
starting childcare Robert had become a knowledgeable operator within the rules
of ownership of centre equipment known to his peers. There is also some evidence
that he was developing an awareness that, under some conditions, rules could be
challenged. In working out the rules Robert appeared to take his cue from the
behaviour and responses of his peers as well as the reactions of the teachers.

Interacting with the physical environment

The story in this section is Shirley's story of 'conquering the slide'. The slide was
an indoor structure that had two flights of steps and two landings. The top landing
was the platform on which children sat down to use the slide.

Shirley first took an interest in the slide during her third orientation visit when
she started to climb up the steps. Her mother, Deborah, noted that Shirley had
never climbed stairs before attending childcare and guided Shirley into the safe
way of climbing first the bottom flight of steps and then the top. However, when
Shirley reached the top and approached the slide, she turned back and climbed
down the steps again. Shirley showed no further interest in either the steps or the
slide during this and the following visit.

In the second week of Shirley's sole attendance, however, climbing the steps
unaided became a challenge to which she returned throughout the session. This
challenge also seemed part of another goal: getting to the top of the slide and
sliding down.

Early in the session, Shirley walked to the bottom of the slide. She watched as other children climbed up and slid down. 'Do you want to go up the stairs Shirley?' asked Joan, a teacher, as she helped Victor. Shirley watched. She knelt on the bottom part of the slide and looked up at Victor who was now at the top of the slide waiting to slide down. Joan came down the steps and shifted Shirley away from the bottom of the slide so that Victor could slide down without bumping into her. Once Victor had slid down, Shirley immediately reclaimed her place at the bottom of the slide. Cheryll, another teacher, came up to Shirley and helped move her out of the way again saying 'Shirley, can you move over so that the other children can slide down?' Shirley walked off to the steps and competently climbed up the bottom flight and down again. Shirley watched keenly and with clear enjoyment as other children successfully slid down the slide. Cheryll responded: 'It's fun, isn't it?'

For about 10 minutes Shirley seemed to forget the slide but then returned to sit at the bottom of it looking up towards the top. She then climbed up the bottom flight of steps for the second time and then attempted the top flight. However, the top flight of steps posed a problem, Shirley could not lift her leg high enough to climb them. She moved away from the slide. After about an hour the challenge of the slide drew Shirley back again. This time Shirley attempted a different technique to achieve her goal: She walked to the bottom of the slide and tried to clamber up from the bottom end. She stumbled and picked herself up matter-of-factly without looking in the least bit upset.

Three minutes later, Shirley was back trying to climb up the slide from the bottom. For a few minutes she was distracted by some play around the home corner but was soon back at the bottom of the slide. She alternated between going up and down the bottom flight of steps, and clambering up the slide from the bottom. After several attempts to ascend the slide in this fashion, Shirley finally found herself one-third of the way up. This was the farthest Shirley had got all morning and her face beamed as she finally slid down. After this 'momentous' event, Shirley abandoned the slide.

Twenty-five minutes later Shirley returned to the steps. This time, having climbed up the first flight quite easily, she also managed to get on to the first step of the second flight. However, Shirley did not continue with this 'adventure' and when she next approached the slide a few minutes later it was to repeat her earlier climb from the bottom of the slide.

When Shirley's mother, Deborah, arrived at pick-up time, Shirley was again trying to climb up the bottom of the slide. Joan explained that Shirley had spent some time at this activity during the session. In response, Deborah lifted Shirley up in her arms, placed her at the top of the slide and supported her as she slid down. Shirley chuckled with delight and her face lit up. Observing from the side, I volunteered the information to Deborah that Shirley had been practising going up the steps all morning but that she had not managed to climb up the top flight on her own yet. Deborah immediately helped Shirley to climb up the top flight and Shirley slid down laughing.

The crowning moment of the day, was, however to unfold in the next few minutes. As Deborah stopped to chat to Joan again, Shirley wandered off by herself to the steps yet again. I wrote in my field notes:

> As mum and Joan talk, Shirley manages to climb up the final two top steps that had defeated her before – and she comes down the slide triumphantly!! (I get all excited that she has managed this and call out to Deborah and Joan to note this achievement!) Shirley is climbing up the top flight of steps again; mum and Joan turn round and cheer her on. Unfortunately, Shirley stumbles on the first of the top lot of steps and tumbles down. Deborah goes up to help and comfort her and Shirley slides down again, her face a picture of delight.

On this note, Shirley's session ended. During the following weeks, the slide remained an area of sustained activity for Shirley. This story about Shirley interacting with an element in her physical environment illustrates Shirley's learning of new skills and the enjoyment that this occasioned in Shirley as well as in the adults around her, including myself as researcher. The beginning of Shirley's story of 'conquering the slide' emerged as a self-directed action on Shirley's part. However, Deborah and Joan soon became tuned in to Shirley's focus of attention and they provided Shirley with both verbal cues and physical assistance to help her climb the steps and use the slide.

The cameos from Shirley's and Robert's experiences are clearly quite different. However, in both cases the children interacted with adults and other children in a process that Rogoff *et al.* (1993) would call 'guided participation'. In this process, children's development is seen to occur through children's 'active participation in culturally structured activity with the guidance, support, and challenge of companions who vary in skill and status' (p. 5). Rogoff *et al.* noted: 'we assume that children advance their understanding in a creative process in which they transform their understanding and become more responsible participants in the practices of their communities as they participate' (p. 6).

Implications for enhancing the experience of starting childcare

I have argued that when the experience of starting childcare is explored as a lived reality, it becomes clear that the traditional focus on this as one of separation does not do justice to the complexity of the event. Beyond the emotional significance of separation, starting childcare emerged in my study as an experience of induction: mothers and children were inducted into a new setting with all its established ways of doing things. In this process both teachers and the established children at the centre acted as agents of induction. Furthermore, my study showed that the teachers made a difference to the quality of the starting childcare experience of all the participants.

With these understandings, it is possible to draw some tentative implications for enhancing the starting childcare experience.

At the level of the childcare setting

The mothers' narratives about what they valued about their starting childcare experience suggest that for mothers this experience could be helped by:

- receiving clear information and guidance about the centre and its daily operation, including specific information about settling-in procedures;
- having printed, as well as oral, information about settling-in;
- having a specific teacher to regularly communicate with about their child;
- receiving regular feedback about their child;
- having their preferred way of handling their child respected;
- seeing their suggestions about their child taken up by the teacher/s;
- being given information on how structural issues about the management of the centre (e.g. teacher : child ratios) ensured that their child received appropriate attention;
- interactions with the centre staff which reassured them about the trustworthiness of the teachers.

From the children's perspective, the data suggest that their experience could be enhanced when:

- they are actively helped to 'fit in' by adults and peers who tune in to their focus of attention;
- teachers are pro-active in approaching a new child during the settling-in period.

The teachers' practices suggest that it is important for teachers:

- to be aware of the impact of their practices on how new children and new parents become inducted into the ways of the centre;
- to be aware of strategies that would ease the mothers', or other home adults', experiences during the settling-in time.

Finally it seems important that, at the level of teacher education and/or professional development, teacher guidance on how to handle this first transition from home to early childhood setting does justice to the complexity of all the participants' experience: a focus on separation is not enough.

Note

This chapter is a development on an address most recently given as part of the international early childhood symposium held at the University of Malta in November 2000.

References

Ainslie, R. and Anderson, C. (1984) 'Day care children's relationships to their mothers and caregivers: an inquiry into the conditions for the development of attachment'. In R. Ainslie (ed.), *The Child and the Daycare Setting*. New York: Praeger.

Ayers, W. (1989) *The Good Pre-school Teacher.* New York: Teachers College Press.

Bailey, B. (1992) '"Mommy, don't leave me!" Helping toddlers and parents deal with separation', *Dimensions of Early Childhood* 20(3), 25–39.

Balaban, N. (1985) *Starting School: From Separation to Independence.* New York: Teachers College Press.

Barraclough, S. and Smith, A.B. (1996) 'Do parents choose and value quality childcare in New Zealand?', *International Journal of Early Years Education* 4(1), 5–26.

Blatchford, P., Battle, S. and Mays, J. (1984) *The First Transition.* Guildford: NFER-Nelson.

Bradbard, M. and Endsley, R. (1980) 'The importance of educating parents to be discriminating day care consumers'. In S. Kilmer (ed.), *Advances in Early Education and Day Care: A Research Annual*, Vol. 1. Greenwich, CT: JAI Press.

Bretherton, I. and Waters, E. (eds) (1985) 'Growing points of attachment theory and research', *Monographs of the Society for Research in Child Development* 50(1–2), (Serial No. 209). Chicago, IL: University of Chicago Press.

Dalli, C. (2000) 'Starting childcare: what young children learn about relating to adults in the first weeks of starting childcare', *Early Childhood Research and Practice* 2(2). Also available online: http://ecrp.uiuc.edu/v2n2/dalli.html.

Daniel, J. (1998) 'A modern mother's place is wherever her children are: facilitating infant and toddler mothers' transitions in child care', *Young Children* 53(6), 4–12.

Farquhar, S.E. (1991) 'Parents as discerning consumers at three types of early childhood centres'. Paper presented at the New Zealand Association for Research in Education 13th National Conference, Dunedin, New Zealand.

Feldbaum, C.L., Christenson, T.E. and O'Neal, E. (1980) 'An observational study of the assimilation of the newcomer to the pre-school', *Child Development* 51, 497–507.

Janis, M. (1964) *A Two-year-old Goes to Nursery School: A Case-study of Separation Reactions.* London: Tavistock Press.

Johnston, A. and Brennan, L. (1997) 'The cry of a baby'. Paper presented at the Australian Early Childhood Association Conference, Melbourne, Australia.

McCartney, K. and Phillips, D. (1988) 'Motherhood and child care'. In B. Birns and D.F. Hay (eds), *The Different Faces of Motherhood.* New York: Plenum Press.

Marcus, J., Chess, S. and Thomas, A. (1972) 'Temperamental individuality in group care of young children', *Early Child Development and Care* 1, 313–30.

Meltzer, D. (1984) 'A one-year-old goes to nursery: A parable of confusing times', *Journal of Child Psychotherapy* 10, 89–104.

Mobley, C. and Pullis, M. (1991) 'Temperament and behavioral adjustment in pre-school children', *Early Childhood Research Quarterly* 6, 577–86.

Murton, A. (1971) *From Home to School.* New York: Citation Press.

Petrie, A.J. and Davidson, I. (1995) 'Toward a grounded theory of parent pre-school involvement', *Early Child Development and Care* 111, 5–17.

Polkinghorne, D. (1995) 'Narrative configuration in qualitative analysis'. In J.A. Hatch and R. Wisniewski (eds), *Life History and Narrative*. London: Falmer Press.

Pramling, I. and Lindahl, M. (1991) 'Awareness and the life-world. Infants' first experience in pre-school'. Paper presented at the 10th International Human Science Research Conference, Göteborg, Sweden.

Pramling, I. and Lindahl, M. (1994) 'Learning from the toddler's perspective in the context of day-care'. Paper presented at the 4th European Conference on the Quality of Early Childhood Education, Göteborg, Sweden

Renwick, M. (1989) *Keeping in Touch. Teachers and Parents in Kindergartens*. Wellington: NZCER.

Robbins, J. (1997) 'Separation anxiety: a study on commencement at pre-school', *Australian Journal of Early Childhood* 22(1), 12–17.

Rogoff, B., Mistry, J., Göncü, A. and Mosier, C. (1993) 'Guided participation in cultural activity by toddlers and caregivers', *Monograph of the Society for Research in Child Development* 58(8), (Serial No. 236). Chicago, IL: University of Chicago Press.

Rolfe, S., Lloyd-Smith, J. and Richards, L. (1991) 'Understanding the effects of infant day care: the case for qualitative study of mothers' experiences', *Australian Journal of Early Childhood* 16(2), 24–32.

Shinn, M.B., Galinsky, E. and Gulcur, L. (1990) *The Role of Childcare Centers in the Lives of Parents*. New York: Families and Work Institute.

Thyssen, S. (2000) 'The child's start in daycare', *Early Child Development and Care* 161, 33–46.

Valsiner, J. (1985) 'Parental organization of children's cognitive development within the home environment', *Psychologia* 28, 131–43.

Valsiner, J. and Hill, P.E. (1989) 'Socialization of American toddlers for social courtesy'. In J. Valsiner (ed.), *Child Development in Cultural Context*. Toronto: Hogrefe and Huber.

Chapter 4

Communication and continuity in the transition from kindergarten to school

Stig Broström

A child's entry into school has long been associated with special expectations and excitement, as well as varying degrees of tension and anxiety. International research on school-start calls attention to the rapid and often unanticipated changes children face in a compressed period of time when they begin school (Margetts, 2000). Parents and teachers recognise the importance of helping children make smooth transitions into school. Smooth school transitions help children feel secure, relaxed, and comfortable in their new environments. A fundamental goal of a school-start transition is to help young children feel *suitable* in school, that is, to have a feeling of well being and belonging.

Children feel 'suitable' when they successfully negotiate the daily challenges of kindergarten life, including both social (peer related) and academic (content related) challenges. Feeling suitable is crucial to the child's learning and development, as well as to a fundamental and continuous sense of well being. Research on school start shows that children who feel suitable, relaxed, and well adjusted in kindergarten are much more likely than children who do not feel well adjusted to experience school success beyond kindergarten (Thompson, 1975; Ladd and Preice, 1987). Much research on school start has focused on teachers' and parents' views of children's skills and knowledge at school entry: that is, an interest to define the concept of school readiness (e.g. Pianta and McCoy, 1997; Lewit and Baker, 1995).

It is important for parents, kindergarten class teachers, and especially kindergarten teachers, to have a shared understanding of the school readiness concept and to agree on what kinds of knowledge, skills and behaviour are prerequisite to a child's likely success in his or her first year of school. However, because research predominantly presents the adult perspective, it can lead to a limited definition of readiness and to adult-centred rather than child-centred or balanced approach to school transition. Consequently smooth and successful transition from kindergarten to school requires attention to several related elements:

- Child readiness or the extent to which the child has developed personal, social and intellectual competence which adults view as necessary for success in the first year of school. Children, who are not deemed 'ready,' especially by their teachers in the first year of school, will be less likely to feel well suited to the environment or capable of meeting its expectations.

- Support from parents, family and community. Adults must be equipped to help the child with all aspects of the new experience, including academic, social, and psychological.
- A system of high quality kindergartens for children aged three to five, which provides a rich daily life carrying its own reward. This includes learning and development as essential ingredients, along with satisfying peer interactions, engaging interactions between children and adults and meaningful play opportunities
- Not only do the children need to be 'school ready', but even more, kindergarten class needs to be 'child ready'. That is, the teacher and the environment created must take the child's perspectives, interests and needs into account. Environment here refers not only to the physical environment, which must include appropriate materials for instruction and play, but also to the psychological environment, which must assist children in developing a sense of 'suitability' for kindergarten, a feeling of belonging, well-being, and capacity to succeed in this new place.
- A critical aspect of being 'child ready' is the school's approach to helping children make the transition from home or kindergarten to school. Such a child ready approach is called 'ready school' in the US document Ready Schools National Education Goals Panel (1998), which among other things stipulated the need for continuity in curricula, home-school communication, and a welcoming environment for family and children.

These related elements, taken together, provide direction for the development of activities on transition, which, when undertaken by families, kindergartens and school, combine the most important areas in the child's life before and after starting school and support the transition. Connections between families, schools, kindergarten, and communities are highlighted in an ecological model or perspective: examples of such models in the American context are described in Pianta and Walsh (1996). They emphasise positive connections between home, kindergarten, and school that are based on personal contact prior to school entry followed by ongoing communication concerning curriculum and activities. Such transition activities have increased rapidly in recent years in Denmark. In the USA Ramey and Ramey (1998) refer to the transition question as a 'hot topic', and Love et al. (1992) reported that roughly 20 per cent of US schools have a range of transition activities that meet the needs of families and students for information about and personal contact with the school.

Problems to overcome

Most children have predominantly positive experiences when they enter school. They meet new academic and social challenges. These challenges mobilise the potentials, the skills and talents the children bring with them to school. However, for some children, starting school is a less than positive experience. For these children, each day brings too many challenges or the wrong kinds of challenges. In spite of all good intentions several typical problems remain:

- Kindergarten teachers have limited knowledge of what happens in kindergarten class in school. Many have a diffuse orientation concerning activities in school or they think school has not changed since their own school time. Kindergarten teachers often express a view that in school children are seated the whole day. They often suggest that learning in school is laborious, while learning in kindergarten is free and playful.
- Similarly, in Denmark kindergarten class teachers' understanding of life in kindergarten is vague. First of all, they see kindergarten as a place where children are mostly cared for in a custodial sense, but not as an educational culture analogous to 'real' school. It is interesting to note here that during the last five to seven years, Danish kindergarten teachers have begun to produce written activity plans, which, seen collectively, represent their own 'curriculum'. However, specific learning goals and outcomes often remain buried within these plans. For example, many teachers write plans including general references to the value of play ('children develop themselves through play'), but they seldom describe how or what the children will learn through play.
- In general, kindergarten class teachers often claim that school starters lack basic skills and competencies they need for success in school. The criticism is that life in kindergarten does not contribute to the level of development necessary for being able to make use of the learning environment in kindergarten class. In other words too many children have not obtained the necessary level of school readiness.
- Kindergarten teachers and kindergarten class teachers have different definitions of school readiness (Hains et al., 1989). Kindergarten teachers seem to stress personal development, action competence, and general skills, whereas the teachers in kindergarten class weight children's abilities to adjust school, to fit in with the other children, and to function in class (Perry et al., 2000).
- Among parents there is an increasing tendency to enrol children too early in kindergarten class, which results in too many children without basic skills and sufficient personal development. Earlier international investigations (e.g. Mortimore et al., 1988; Russel and Startrup, 1986) show that young school starters, compared with children a few months older, have more behaviour and learning problems. However, the literature is mixed with regard to the lasting effects of a poor school start. A Danish study indicated that children with problems in school start often have problems later in school. On the other hand, an Australian longitudinal investigation of 698 children did not confirm this finding.
- Educational contradictions between today's kindergarten and kindergarten class are significant (Broström, 1998, 1999). In Denmark kindergarten is child oriented with an emphasis on play and practical-aesthetic activities. In kinder-

garten class activities are more teacher-directed, and besides play and practical-aesthetic activities the three R's are implemented. Kindergarten classes in school are rooted in a shared historical, educational, and ideological tradition. As recently as the early 1990s, kindergarten classes were very similar to kindergarten (Broström, 1998). However, during the last decade, fundamental differences in educational goals, content and principles may have emerged. The common practice in kindergarten to day seems to stress play and to de-emphasise creative-aesthetic activities as well as the teachers' active role in supporting learning. By contrast a school-like curriculum is often seen in today's kindergarten class (Broström, 1999).

- There is a lack of communication between kindergarten teachers and teachers from kindergarten class in the period leading up to children's transition. Thus the teachers from kindergarten class meet the children without prior knowledge about the individual children or the group as a whole. This lack of communication is particularly disturbing with regard to children at risk, since the kindergarten class teachers are unable to prepare the additional support needed for them to enter school successfully.

- In a recent study it was found that some of the kindergarten children had diffuse expectations or no expectations about what they would experience in kindergarten class. However, 75 per cent of the children reported a correlation between what they expected when they entered kindergarten class and what they actually experienced.

- This study also revealed that some children had an outdated picture of the school as a place where children have to sit down and behave quietly or the teacher will scold and smack. Children with such a view are at high risk from school-related anxiety and nervousness. This can drain children's energy to such an extent that they can't mobilise their existing skills and talents on their own behalf when they enter school. From this perspective, we might say that such children are not ready for school. A Danish study from 1995 of 565 five- to six-year-old children's expectations about the first year of school shows that 12 per cent seemed to be marked by insecurity and nervousness. A parallel investigation in spring 1999 of 375 five- to six-year-old kindergarten children's expectations about school shows a similar or heightened tendency. Here 24 per cent expressed an expectation characterised by a scolding teacher, who commands children to sit still and be quiet. More problematic is the fact that among the anxiety-answers, 5 per cent of the children expected to meet an *authoritarian* school in which the teacher has power and uses his power to oppress children. Probably these children are nervous starting school. However, recent research presents mixed views on whether most children look forward to starting school. According to one Norwegian study (Lillemyr, 2001) a third of six- to seven-year-old children feared starting school. However, German research with 162 children produced different results, indicating that kinder-garten children have generally positive attitudes about school and look forward to starting kindergarten class (Griebel and Niesel, 1999). A major difference in the German study and the Nordic studies mentioned is that the German study asked children more directly about their positive and negative views. Perhaps Danish children would also express more positive expectations if the interviews were reconstructed to solicit them.

Transition activities

The problems described above, especially some children's fear for school, advocate for the establishment of transition activities, which will bring greater continuity to children's lives as they move from kindergarten into the first few years of formal education in school. This implies that parents, kindergarten teachers, kindergarten class teachers, grade 1 and 2 teachers, and leisure-time teachers work in close co-operation. During the last decade, educators in many countries have made concerted efforts to build such collaborations among kindergarten and primary teachers as well parents of children entering school. New investigations show that such a developed relationship and ongoing communication is pivotal for a good start in school (Pianta andWalsh, 1996; Christenson, 1999; Epstein, 1996).

International literature and reports from practice describe in detail various approaches to school transition. Most approaches emphasise both kindergartens that help children become school ready (school ready kindergartens) and child-ready schools. Among other things, *school ready kindergartens* develop curriculum and instructional practices which, on the one hand, meet the child's interest, and have their own value, and, on the other hand, foster an appropriate educational culture to help children become school ready. Thus there is a co-ordination of and continuity between the kindergarten and school curriculum. Here recent research advocates for developmentally based practice with play, co-operative roles, and social interaction with other children as the foundation for comprehensive development, as well as the development of skills and abilities more closely related to school readiness (Love *et al.*, 1992).

Child ready schools meet children as they are. Through meetings with the kindergarten teacher, the kindergarten class teachers gain knowledge about the individual child, relations between children, and group dynamics. Another strategy, which helps kindergarten class teachers become more familiar with each new group of children is for the kindergarten teacher to forward photographs, drawings, and favourite stories from the kindergarten.

Children cope better in situations when they receive support from teachers and parents as well as from peers whom they view as friends (Ladd, 1990). Therefore, teachers can create classrooms that are secure bases for incoming school starters by building upon children's previously existing friendships. Especially in the first few weeks in the new school setting, many children are more willing to handle and explore new challenges when they can hold a friend's hand, both literally and figuratively (Griebel and Niesel, 1999). Compared to children without friends, children with friends in the classroom during the first weeks developed more positive views of school (Ladd, 1990). The importance of proximity to a friend can be explained in the light of the fact, that especially in a situation characterised by changes, people seek continuity (Bronfenbrenner, 1986; Fabian, 1998; Griebel and Niesel, 1999).

In Denmark during the period 1998 to 2000, we have seen a cascade of transition activities, including those mentioned briefly above, the different kind of teachers have developed many variations on the themes of mutual visits and collaborations between home and school. It seems obvious that such transition practices should prove to be beneficial for children, teachers, and parents. At first sight, it may also appear that systematic and appropriate transition schemes should be relatively easy to implement. In fact, however, such transition practices are both time consuming and problematic. Barriers include lack of time and resources in general. However, perhaps the most salient and challenging barrier often goes unacknowledged: differences in the educational traditions and understandings of kindergarten teachers and school teachers often makes it difficult for them to communicate and co-operate in actual practice. However, in spite of these hindrances, teachers still seem to have an optimistic view of the challenges and possibilities associated with developing school transition schemes.

Teachers understanding of transition activities

To gain knowledge about teachers' understanding of and attitudes about school transition practice, the author developed a questionnaire survey in which teachers were asked to reflect on and judge a numbers of transition activities. Included in the study were kindergarten teachers, kindergarten class teachers, teachers from grades 1 and 2, and leisure-time teachers. The survey was based on an extensive review of literature on transition to school, an American survey conducted by the National Transition Study (Love *et al.*, 1992), an American survey involving 3,595 kindergarten teachers (Pianta *et al.*, 1999), and a Danish evaluation study on transition activities.

Method

The questionnaire reflected the overall goals of kindergarten transition practices, as well as barriers to these practices. The questionnaire consisted of a list of typical transition activities, which the respondents were asked to judge as 'good idea' or 'not'. In addition, respondents were asked to comment if they saw any problems or barriers related to the implementation of the 'good idea' practice. Unlike the study conducted by Pianta *et al.* (1999), the present study did not use a list of potential barriers, but asked the respondents to formulate possible barriers themselves.

A pilot study was conducted with thirty kindergarten teachers, kindergarten class teachers, teachers, and leisure-time teachers, in order to obtain a more precise wording for survey items and also to assist in constructing additional questions.

Ultimately, the questionnaire consisted of questions about 32 transition activities. The questionnaires were distributed to kindergarten teachers, kindergarten class teachers, grade 1 and 2 teachers, and leisure-time teachers through the administrations in four municipalities near Copenhagen. In addition, questionnaires were also distributed to similar groups in some villages. About 600 questionnaires were distributed and 249 were completed and returned. The data were analyzed using SPSS, a computer programme designed for complex sample surveys.

Reading the completed questionnaires, some sources of error appeared. Although it seemed clear that the questionnaire asked for a judgement of each transition activity, some respondents seemed to answer whether they have made use of the particular transition practice or not. Therefore, some responses are probably a mixture of attitudes and practice. However, all answers were recorded as a judgement, that is, as the respondent's attitude to the transition activity.

Results

Table 4.1 expresses in percentage how 249 school teachers, kindergarten teachers, kindergarten class teachers, leisure-time teachers judge 32 transitions activities to 'be a good idea'.

All types of teachers expressed a generally positive attitude to transition activities. They found it is a good idea to have meetings, mutual visits and some shared activities. However, with regard to a co-ordination of the two curricula (number 26) and co-ordinated teaching (number 27) only about 60 per cent of the teachers judged these as 'a good idea'. Though this percentage is not disastrously low, it suggests resistance to bridging the two educational traditions. This finding is in concert with an earlier study (Broström, 1999) showing some educational contradictions between kindergarten and kindergarten classes in school. In view of these contradictions, one might expect to see a certain level of aversion to incorporating the other's tradition. Various kinds of teachers who responded to the survey in the current study were more positive about meetings, discussions and mutual visits, all of which they viewed as important and fruitful. However, their responses indicated some hesitation when questions involved collaboration on curriculum and teaching methods.

All types of teachers surveyed expressed a distinct understanding of and interest in nearly all of the transition activities. However, because there are some educational contradictions between kindergarten, leisure-time centre and school, data were analyzed to determine whether teachers from these various settings and traditions judge transition activities differently.

Difference between different types of teachers

On most items, there were no appreciable differences in responses from the various types of teachers (kindergarten teacher, kindergarten class teachers, grades 1 and

Table 4.1 Percentage of 249 kindergarten teachers, kindergarten class teachers, leisure-time teachers, and grade 1 and 2 teachers judging transitions activities to 'be a good idea'

Transition activity	Percentage
1 The school invites the child to visit the class before school start	95.9
2 The kindergarten teachers and children visit the class before school start	93.4
3 The kindergarten teachers and children visit leisure-time centre	93.1
4 The next year teacher has some time in kindergarten class	92.3
5 Talk with parents after school start	90.0
6 Kindergarten teachers and kindergarten class teachers have conferences before school start about children's life and development	89.9
7 Letters to parents before school start	89.3
8 Flyers to parents before school start	87.6
9 The teacher team in kindergarten class is made up of kindergarten class teachers and grade 1 and 2 teachers	86.5
10 Letters to children before school start	85.2
11 Open house in kindergarten class before school start	84.9
12 Some teaching periods are co-ordinated between kindergarten class, grades 1 and 2, and leisure-time centre	83.9
13 Meetings with children and parents before school start	83.0
14 Talks with parents before school start	82.0
15 Co-operation with parents are co-ordinated between school and leisure-time centre	81.9
16 Kindergarten, school and leisure-time centre read each other's curriculum, activity plans, and other written documents	80.1
17 Kindergarten class teachers visit their incoming students in their kindergartens	79.8
18 Leisure-time teachers are a part of the teacher team in school	79.2
19 The kindergarten class teacher follows the children to grade 1, either some lessons during the week or integrated in the teacher team	78.3
20 The school invites the eldest children from the nearby kindergartens to participate in cultural events at the school	77.6
21 At school enrolment children and parents meet the kindergarten class teacher	77.6
22 Currently teachers and kindergarten class teachers visit each other and observe the educational practice	77.2
23 Kindergarten teachers, kindergarten class teachers, teachers and leisure-time teachers have shared meetings to discuss education	76.0
24 Letters to parents after school start	71.1
25 Before school start kindergarten and kindergarten class have shared meeting with the parents	65.7
26 Co-ordinated curriculum between kindergarten, kindergarten class, and leisure-time centre	60.3
27 Co-ordinated teaching between kindergarten, kindergarten class, and leisure-time centre	59.4
28 Open house in kindergarten class after school start	52.8
29 Flyer to parents after school start	41.1
30 Home visit after school start	40.0
31 Letters to children after school start	39.6
32 Home visit before school start	27.5

2 teachers, and leisure-time teachers). However, significant differences did appear on responses to a few specific transition activities.

As illustrated in Table 4.2 kindergarten teachers seem to be less positive about transition activities concerning reading each other's documents, having shared meetings on educational practice, and a co-ordination of the curriculum (numbers 16, 23 and 26). Kindergarten teachers showed reluctance to consider a co-ordinated curriculum: probably they were worried that the result of such collaboration would be the implementation of a more school-oriented curriculum at the kindergarten level.

However, leisure-time teachers responded much more positively to the idea of co-ordinating the curriculum (number 26). This group's positive judgement on this item is rather surprising, since leisure-time teachers often express a not-school-like attitude. Interestingly, leisure-time teachers gave a low priority to 'have shared meetings to discuss education'. One reasonable explanation for this seeming contradiction is that leisure-time teachers want to co-ordinate the curriculum, but they do not want to spend hours and hours in meetings to accomplish this goal.

While kindergarten teachers showed low interest in transitions activities 16, 23 and 26 (Table 4.2), they gave a high priority to transition activity number 25: 'before school start kindergarten and kindergarten class have shared meetings with parents'. Yet in a way it is surprising not all kindergarten teachers think it is important to have a opportunity to inform parents of life in kindergarten class in order to establish realistic expectations.

Table 4.2 Distribution of four types of teacher's positive judgement ('good idea') of some transition activities (%)

Transition activity	Kindergarten teachers	Kindergarten class teachers	School teachers	Leisure-time teachers
16. Reading each other's curriculum and other written documents	72	82	80	88
23. Having shared meetings to discuss education	52	84	79	46
26. Co-ordinated curriculum between kindergarten, kindergarten class, and leisure-time centre	37	66	70	76
25. Before school start kindergarten and kindergarten class have shared meetings with parents	92	76	76	71

Note:
The numbers in the left hand column refer to the numbers in Table 4.1.

Difference between Danish and American teachers' judgments

As mentioned above, the Danish survey was inspired by an American survey involving 3,595 kindergarten teachers (Pianta *et al.*, 1999). The similar origins and intentions of the two studies make it possible to compare the findings to a certain extent.

The American questionnaire consisted of 23 transition activities. In the development of the Danish questionnaire 20 questions from the survey by Pianta *et al.* (1999) were used. The addition of 12 more questions were necessary to reflect new transition practices in Denmark and problems associated with these practices.

Generally speaking, we find no dramatic differences or contradictions between Danish and American teachers' judgments of transition activities. However, differences appear on activity 26 'co-ordinated curriculum between kindergarten, kindergarten class and leisure-time centre. Here only 60 per cent Danish teachers as opposed to 85 per cent of US teachers want such a co-ordination. Perhaps American kindergarten teachers and school teachers have fewer disagreements about curricula at their respective levels than Danish teachers do. If this is true, then, representing Danish perspectives and debates, Danish teachers would likely question whether the American kindergarten is expected to adjust to the demands of the school when they 'collaborate' about curricula.

Regardless of the generally positive attitudes toward transition activities among all types of Danish teachers, there is obviously a distance between positive attitudes and actual implementation of effective and appropriate transition practices. Many barriers and hindrances appear when kindergarten teachers, kindergarten class teachers, grade 1 and 2 teachers, and leisure-time teachers attempt to co-operate in order to bridge kindergarten, school and leisure-time centre.

Barriers

In the evaluation report of the project 'A good start in school', conducted by the Danish Ministry of Education, most of the above-mentioned transition activities were used and positively described. Although all types of teachers generally found these activities very satisfactory, they also reported a series of problems, hindrances, and barriers.

To gain more knowledge about barriers, the Danish questionnaire invited the respondents to describe possible problems and barriers concerning the implementation. It was expected that the respondents would indicate a large number of barriers, which would make it difficult to carry through the mentioned transition activities. Strangely enough, only a small percentage of the respondents remarked on this topic. Actually, spread among the 32 transition activities, only 70 respondents made comments concerning possible barriers.

How can that be understood? Does it mean than Danish teachers have no problems with transition activities? Do they have enough resources, and do they find it easy to co-operate with colleagues with another educational traditions and backgrounds? This does not seem very probable. This is not what teachers used to say. Possibly the respondents did not want to spend the time to fill out that part of the survey? Although data from this study on barriers are limited, responses do signal some of the likely hindrances to successful school transitions, for example lack of time, difference in educational cultures, professional demarcations between various types of teachers, and borders related to union policy.

The above-mentioned barriers are real, and should not be interpreted only as reluctance and aversion by teachers. In order to bridge kindergarten, school and leisure-time centre, it is necessary to add resources to the field. If such resources are not forthcoming, there is a risk that the wide range of emergent transition activities will simply die off before they have a chance to succeed. Good intentions alone will not be sufficient to ensure the implementation of appropriate activities that will give all children an opportunity of transition to the new world that awaits them through the school house door.

References

Bronfenbrenner, U. (1986) 'Recent advances in research on ecology of human develop-ment'. In Silbereisen, R.K., Eyfeth, K. and Rudintger, G. (eds), *Development as Action in Context. Problem Behaviour and Normal Youth Development*. Berlin: Springer.

Broström, S. (1998) 'Kindergarten in Denmark and the USA', *Scandinavian Journal of Educational Research* 42(2), 109–22.

Broström, S. (1999) 'Changes in early childhood education in Denmark. The appearance of literacy in early childhood education'. In Brougére, G. and Rayna, S. (ed.), *Culture, Enfance et Éducation Préscolaire. (Culture, Childhood and Preschool Education)*. Paris: Université Paris-Nord and INRP. UNESCO.

Broström, S. (2001) 'Constructing the early childhood curriculum: the example of Denmark'. In David, T. (ed.), *Promoting Evidence-based Practice in Early Childhood Education: Research and Implications*. London: JAI (in press).

Christenson, S.L. (1999) 'Critical issues for families and schools: rights, responsibilities, resources, and relationship'. In Pianta, R.C. and Cox, M.J. (eds), *The Transition to Kindergarten: Research, Policy, Practice and Training*. Baltimore: Paul Brookes.

Epstein, J.L. (1996) 'Advances in family, community, and school partnerships', *New Schools, New Communities* 12(3), 5–13.

Fabian, H. (1998) 'Developing a conceptual framework for children's induction to reception class and their transitions through school'. Paper presented at EECERA 8th European Conference on Quality in Early Childhood Education. Santiago de Compostella, Spain.

Griebel, W. and Niesel, R. (1999) 'From kindergarten to school: a transition for the family'. Paper presented at the EECERA 9th European Conference on Quality in Early Child-hood Education. Helsinki.

Hains, A.H., Fowler, S.A., Schwartz, I.S., Kottwiz, E. Rosenkotter, S. (1989) 'A comparison of preschool and kindergarten teacher expectations for school readiness', *Early Childhood Research Quarterly* 4, 75–88.

Ladd, G.W. (1990) 'Having friends, keeping friends, making friends, and being liked by peers, in the classroom: predictors of children's early school adjustment?', *Child Development* 61, 1081–100.

Ladd, G.W. and Preice, J.M. (1987) 'Predicting children's social and school adjustment following the transition from pre-school to kindergarten', *Child Development* 58, 1168–89.

Lewit, E.M. and Baker, L.S. (1995) 'School readiness', *The Future of Children* 52(2), 128–39.

Lillemyr, O.F. (2001) 'Play and learning in school: a motivational approach'. In McInterney, D. and Van Etten, S. (eds), *Research on Sociocultural Influences on Motivation and Learning*. Greewich, CT: Information Age Publishing Inc.

Love, J.M., Logue, M.E., Trudeau, J.V. and Thayer, K. (1992) *Transitions to Kindergarten in American Schools*. Portsmouth: US Department of Education.

Margetts, K. (2000) 'Indicators of children's adjustment to the first year of schooling', *Journal of Australian Research in Early Childhood Education* 7(1), 20–30.

Mortimore, P., Sammons, P., Stroll, L., Lewis, D. and Ecom, R. (1988) *School Matters*. Welss: Open Books.

National Educational Goals Panel (1989) *Ready Schools*. Washington, DC: Author.

Perry, B., Dockett, S. and Howard, P. (2000) 'Starting school: issues for children, parents and teachers', *Journal of Australian Research in Early Childhood Education* 7(1), 44–53.

Pianta, R.C. and McCoy, S.J. (1997) 'The first day of school: the predictive validity of early school screening', *Journal of Applied Developmental Psychology* 18, 1–22.

Pianta, R.C. and Walsh, D.J. (1996) *High-risk-children in Schools: Constructing, Sustaining Relationship*. New York: Routledge.

Pianta, R.C., Cox, M.J., Taylor, L. and Early, D. (1999) 'Kindergarten teacher' practices related to the transition to school: results of national survey', *The Elementary School Journal* 100(1), 71–86.

Ramey, S.L. and Ramey, C.T. (1998) 'The transition to school: opportunities and challenges for children, families, educators, and communities', *The Elementary School Journal* 98(4), 293–5.

Russel, R.J.H. and Startrup, M.J. (1986) 'Month of birth and academic achievement', *Personality and Individual Difference* 7, 839–46.

Thompson, B. (1975) 'Adjustment to school', *Education Quarterly* 17(2), 128–36.

Chapter 5

Co-constructing transition into kindergarten and school by children, parents and teachers

Wilfried Griebel and Renate Niesel

Theoretical background: multi-perspective transition approach of family development in a life-long perspective

Earlier German studies on entry into kindergarten either referred to attachment theory (Laewen, 1989), to Erickson's developmental theory (Berger, 1997) or to stress theory (Haefele and Wolf-Filsinger, 1986), whilst study of entry into school, the eco-psychological perspective, that is the person–process–context model of Bronfenbrenner (1979) was used. Interactions of a child in different social systems and interactions among these systems is described, school is understood as a micro-system, connecting school with the child's family, with school working as a meso-system (Nickel, 1990; Petzold, 1992). Societal norms and values work within a macro-system level. Transition into secondary school was studied by Sirsch (2000) in Vienna within a framework of advanced stress theory including the appraisal of stress (Lazarus and Folkman, 1987). In a new study on the transitions of children into and between institutions, namely kindergarten, elementary school and secondary school, Beelmann (2001) bases his work on Bronfenbrenner's model as well as on Filipp's (1995) conceptualisation of critical life events and of norma-tive social transitions (Olbrich, 1995). These life events can stimulate development in a positive way, but under adverse conditions in a way that is disadvantageous to the child. Reactions of children in transitions have been described as developmental disharmonies rather than stress reactions (Kienig, 1998). Fabian (1998) integrates an anthropological approach drawing on van Gennep (1960) in her conceptual framework, describing rites of passage for entering the school system. Within a developmental perspective of adaptation to changes in life circumstances, Welzer (1993) defines transition as a phase of intensified and accelerated developmental demands, that are socially regulated. Children learn special competencies in the 'dual socialisation' of family and institution (Dencik, 1997).

In our society, children and their families will have to cope with more and more discontinuities and transitions in their lives, for example, parental divorce and remarriage (Fthenakis, 1998). From our background as family researchers, we found Cowan's (1991) concept of family transition – originally designed to study the birth of the first child, divorce and remarriage – a suitable vehicle for understanding the multiple demands and expectations concerning children entering kindergarten (Griebel and Niesel, 1997; Niesel and Griebel, 2000). This concept takes into account the perspectives of all family members, and we added the teachers' view. It is developmentally oriented and stresses the meaning of a changing identity. Our study aims at a conceptualisation of pedagogical support in kindergarten and school for children and parents coping with this transition. Our work should be understood as part of a life-long perspective of transition learning.

Transition in our study (Niesel and Griebel, 2000) in a heuristic way is understood as a process leading to changes in:

- identity
- roles
- relations
- settings representatives commuting between different settings.

Methodologically, including the child's perspective into childhood research remains a challenging task (Fuhs, 2000; Heinzel, 2000; Zinnecker, 1996) as well as a rewarding one (Griebel and Niesel, 2000a). New childhood research aims at making social construction of childhood visible (Scholz, 1994). As both children and adults are working together in co-constructing the specific world of childhood, both perspectives have to be considered (Hülst, 2000). Continuing reflection is needed on how to translate the personal world of children without deforming it through the adult's perspective, and vice versa.

Empirical background: two small-scale, quantitative and qualitative studies in Bavaria

Study I (Griebel and Niesel, 1997)

Research questions referred to admission procedures, transition experiences of parents and children, the teacher's recognition of children's and parents adaptation, the dialogue between parents and teachers and exchange of information between the setting and families.

- 133 (44 per cent) of questionnaires for kindergarten teachers in Bavaria were returned. 124 teachers completed an additional part concerning the adaptation of a target child in the group, who was also the first-born child in the family;
- interviews took place with 20 parents at the beginning of kindergarten and six months after entry of their first-born child;
- interviews took place with 11 children in two kindergarten groups, both newcomers and older children together, in small discussion groups.

Study 2 (Griebel and Niesel, 1999, 2000b)

Research questions referred to coping with entry into kindergarten (retrospectively), preparation for school in kindergarten and at home including 'playing school', children's general competencies and coping strategies, expectations of parents and additional transitions in the family:

- questionnaire information on 162 first-born children (85 girls, 77 boys) in Bavaria from parents and from kindergarten educators;
- interview data from 27 of these children at the end of the last kindergarten year, three months after entry into school, half a year after entry into school and at the time of the first report from the school teacher; and
- interview data from parents three months and six months after child's school entry.

Results

Feelings and ideas the children expressed themselves

Transition from family to kindergarten

We gained some detailed insights into the children's perspectives and we found the different areas defined within the transition concept mirrored the children's statements. Even older children remembered entry into kindergarten very well and confirmed the emotional importance of that time. Quotations show the presence of 'mum' in the child's coping efforts to illustrate the co-constructive nature of transition.

The child experiences a qualitative shift in perception of himself or herself, in *identity*. She or he develops a feeling of having a new status and being a competent kindergarten child. The child adds the new *role* of kindergarten child to her/his role as a child in a family.

> I cried a lot, when I was new here. But secretly. Nobody should see that. Because I wanted to be a kindergarten child and I did not want to be one. My head didn't know that. That's what it was like. (Petra, 4:1)

To stay all morning in kindergarten is completely different from a visitor's role.

> I have known for long, what you do and what you don't: hit, bite, scream and bad words. (Wedran, 6:0)

> So I have been here already quite a time, not very long. In the beginning I did not want this, but my mum showed me everything and I could visit them here.

Visiting is better, because I could go home when I wanted to. Now it is over with visits. (Fanny, 3:3)

The child develops new *relationships* with teachers and peers. These relationships reflect what it means to become a kindergarten child. Within the family, relationships change when the child gets more independent.

I don't have a friend. I am looking for one, but Fernando doesn't want to be yet. He would then play with me. (Maxi, 4:0)

So, a kindergarten child must do a lot by himself. And please, not always cry or hit! It works out, if you ask Mrs. K. she will help you. I like to be here because I have good friends, for example Wedran, here. We are a team. What is that? Well, what one doesn't do, the other one does. We help each other, also against the girls. They scream and destroy our constructions. But we take care now, don't we, Wedran? (Marius, 4:9)

Entry to kindergarten means the starting point of *commuting between different settings*. The child adapts to demands that are specific for kindergarten and combines that with demands at home.

So, home is home, and kindergarten is kindergarten. Here is my work and at home is off-time, understand? My mum says work is me learning something. Learning is when you drive your head, and off-time is, when the head slows down. I like that. (David, 3:10)

The tables are different here and the chairs. This many wouldn't fit in my home. I like it when I come here and I like it better, when my mum takes me home again. (Julia, 3:4)

The *nature of the process* means that the transition begins some time before entry into kindergarten and adaptation lasts longer than parents and teachers usually expect.

So, in the beginning everything here was new. But a few days later it was old. Not really old, just for me. You understand? (Toni, 4:1)

Strong emotions accompany the transition process until a new emotional equilibrium is reached. Stress can be eased by adequate coping strategies and if demands are viewed as challenges rather than threats (Lazarus and Folkman, 1987).

When I was still little here, I was so excited. I could not sleep at night. I was happy and I was afraid. Everything was so big and I always walked behind my mum. But she put me in here and – that was it. (Tino, 3:8)

When I was new, I felt very sad. With mum it was so cosy, and here it was so much! (Andi, 4:8)

Transition from kindergarten to school

Before school started, all children were looking forward to school. Some seemed a little anxious about what would come. Their imaginations about what school really means were vague, they did not report much concrete information even if they had visited a school with their kindergarten group. We found some pivotal conceptions by which children gained an understanding about the school life they expected. Some of these are 'learning', 'break-time', 'report' and 'grades'. These representations of school in children's minds seem to be influenced by the culture of kindergarten and by parents as well.

Nine out of ten children visited a school (not necessarily the school, they would attend). But we know very little about what really could be observed there by the children and what they could learn about the school culture. Yet this is considered to be an important prerequisite of preparation for school (Fabian, 1998; Kienig, 1999). Only one out of four children experienced a schoolteacher visiting the children in the kindergarten.

All children were convinced that they would do well at school. They felt supported by parents and by kindergarten teachers. Some children's expectations about school were shaped by messages and narratives from parents about school grades and future life that created achievement pressure.

The children said they were not afraid of older children who might bully them.

After they had attended school for some weeks, children felt that entering school in some ways turned out to be different from what they had expected. They were impressed by the large number of other children in their classroom and in school, they were overwhelmed by the many new impressions. They learned that they *must* do things, whereas before they were allowed to *choose* to do things, and they did not like this difference. All of them were very fond of their teacher whether or not s/he was strict. The children enjoyed learning new things and they felt supported by the teacher.

Some children not only entered school, but simultaneously entered day-care for schoolchildren. Older children in school and day-care were role models for the younger ones. Children sometimes actively sought older children and expected them to protect them from threatening older children. They used these relations as a strategy in coping with transition into school. Day-care seemed to be an important resource for friendships in schools.

Half a year later, the children had acquainted themselves with school demands. They had all made friends there, felt happy but were no longer euphoric. They said that doing homework was a burden to them. When asked what they would like to change, they wanted fewer school hours and more free time in the morning. Some teachers had been replaced by others, and children found that disruptive. They had got their first report from school, had talked about it with their parents and found it accurate and were satisfied with it.

In general they had turned out to be competent schoolchildren who had learned a lot within a transition phase with multiple demands. We asked the children what they thought and felt (*t1*= at the end of kindergarten; *t2* = after two months at school):

Claudia (*t1*)
RESEARCHER: You said before, that you would prefer to stay in kindergarten?
CLAUDIA: Yes, well, but the first day is always beautiful, the second also, but the third not quite.
RESEARCHER: Are you a little bit nervous about it?
CLAUDIA: Well, yeah – I just wait and see.

Claudia (*t2*)
CLAUDIA: My first day in school was just beautiful. Now it is different, it is harder. It was different from what I had thought. But my feeling was good. I just have to be attentive now and you are not allowed to play in school. Only during break. I would like to have school and kindergarten by turns. That would be great.

Karin (*t1*)
RESEARCHER: Next Tuesday you will go to school. Can you imagine how it will be there?
KARIN: Learning … yeah and learn to write … I will have to learn an awful lot.

Karin (*t2*)
RESEARCHER: How do you feel now at school?
KARIN: Hmm, well it was somewhat strange. But it was also great, a great feeling. I started with two friends, so we did not feel so strange.
RESEARCHER: And what is not so good?
KARIN: Homework every day, and that the boys are so wild.

Susanne (*t1*)
RESEARCHER: When you go to school soon, will it be difficult to get up early?
SUSANNE: Then we will just go to bed earlier. It will be more difficult for my parents. Not for me.

Susanne *(t2)*
SUSANNE: In the beginning I was a little bit excited and did not feel quite sure. I thought I felt a little bit of fear … I was just nervous about whether I would get a nice teacher … and in the beginning I was not clever, I did not know the letters, then, only the A.
RESEARCHER: And are you cleverer now?
SUSANNE: Yes, of course, now I know all letters from A to Z.

Differences in parents' and educators' perspectives on school preparation

We found discrepancies in parents' expectations about methods of preparing their children for school on the one hand and the teachers' beliefs about what parents expect for their children on the other hand. Years ago many teachers in kindergartens decided not to use work sheets. Many parents however appreciate this medium, which is commercially available in many forms, to prepare their child for the demands of school. We also found differences in rating the children's competencies at the end of kindergarten. Teachers considered children to be better prepared for school than did their parents. In some cases a child's problem behaviour was evaluated in different ways (Griebel and Niesel, 2000a).

Parent–teacher agreement about children's competencies

The closer the contact between parents and teachers, the less difference there was in their view of children's competencies. Close contact was more important than general kindergarten involvement.

The higher the agreement of parents and teachers about the child, the more optimistic the expectations of parents for the child's school entry.

The less positively parents rated their children's competencies, the less optimistic they were in respect to their child entering school, irrespective of the teacher's rating of that child.

Experiences of parents

At the end of kindergarten, parents, in general, expressed optimism, but also some scepticism and concern. They confirmed that their children were very optimistic about school, that they couldn't wait to get there and enjoyed the idea of being able to read and write very soon. Recalling the first day of school later, parents reported strong emotions, a mixture of joy and pride about their 'big' daughters or sons, but some sadness and feelings of loss as well. They said that a part of untroubled childhood was over. They very often used the phrase that a 'seriousness of life' would start now.

Changes in role expectations

All parents in our study felt a strong sense of responsibility for their child's accomplishments in school from the very beginning (cf. Paetzold, 1988). This was most clearly expressed in parents' involvement in the child's homework.

Homework represents the influence of school on the family. Mothers organised, supervised and supported homework in many ways. Most parents accepted the amount of homework without protest. Fathers liked to be informed about school affairs in the evening, some of them also glanced at the homework and some helped their child with reading practice. In most families doing homework was a main source of conflict as children's enthusiasm for school started to decline when they experienced homework as difficult, time-consuming and shortening playtime.

Parents acted as the school's agents at home. They tried to give a positive representation of school and the teacher at home to keep the children motivated. Before starting school, enhancing children's motivation is considered to be an important way of preparing for the transition (Kienig, 1999). However, some parents also used the teacher and the expectation of failure and criticism as a threat against the children, if they would not obey parental expectations or commands. Sometimes it seems that the mothers are more demanding than teachers (Paetzold, 1988).

In the parents' statements we could identify stages in the process of becoming parents of a schoolchild.

Changes in relationships

The achievement and academic skills of the child became a new field in which the child was confronted with criticism and control. This was a new experience compared to when the child was in kindergarten. A gain in the child's autonomy also changed the relationships with parents. In several aspects the children rejected parental care and control. For example, being allowed to go out alone, make their way to school alone, choose their dress themselves. Some parents said that they were surprised how fast their child had developed, how strong the efforts to gain autonomy were and that it was not always easy for them to let go. Concerns about separation from their children, the safety and care aspects of the setting might cause anxiety, that can be transmitted to the child (Fabian, 1998).

Besides the changes of relationships within the family, parents had to establish some form of relations with the teacher. They had to find a position within the group of parents who sometimes functioned as a support system and as a source of information.

Integrating the demands of two settings: commuting between school and family

Parents experience their child before and after school, teachers experience them after and before family. At home the transition process of becoming a schoolchild is continued. Parents adapt to a family member who is commuting by reorganising the daily routine and labour division. In general the family atmosphere got stricter as new duties were required, and more often something had to be done against the child's wishes. Regularity, even punctuality, gained greater meaning in relation to the child's daily routine. Some parents said that their child was exhausted when he/she came home from school. Mothers sometimes had problems integrating household chores and caring for younger siblings in the morning while the afternoon was to some extent busy with homework.

Changes in identity

In the eyes of their parents, the children had gained in independence during the transition. This reduction of parental care and control is an aspect of gaining a new parental identity as parent of a schoolchild. The parents reported that the children had developed a new picture of themselves as a 'big schoolchild' where they were curious, self-confident and self-assertive. All changes, as they occur in transitions, carry conflicts with them, because changes do not occur simultaneously or harmoniously in all areas.

Parental behaviour as coping strategies with transition

We considered whether parental feelings and behaviours could be interpreted as *coping strategies* that parents employ to support their child's transition from kindergarten child to schoolchild and to master their own transition to being a parent of a schoolchild (Griebel and Niesel, 1999, 2000b).

Before entry into school, s*eeking reassurance* that their child was ready for school was a main endeavour for parents. That the children felt bored by kindergarten activities in the final months and communicated this to parents, was seen by them as a sign of school readiness, supported by some teachers. *Stressing the child's cognitive competencies* more than before, reflected some anticipation of change. By *keeping close contact with the child's kindergarten teacher*, parents gained a more optimistic rating of their child's cognitive and social competencies. Most parents appreciated that their child's age was closer to the seventh than to the sixth birthday at entry into school, expecting better mental and physical readiness.

Seeking continuity was expressed by stressing the importance of friends staying together with their child in the class. This gave continuity of friendships for both the children and their parents, sharing their parental transition efforts. *Information about school(s)* was gathered mostly from other parents with older children.

After entry into school, nearly all parents said that they were lucky with their child's particular teacher, despite the sadness that some parents expressed about the idea that somebody else would get influence over their child. *Developing a positive picture of the teacher* eases the development of a good relationship, which in turn is an important pedagogical topic (Pianta, 1999).

Parents took care to *have a clear structure for the new daily and weekly routine* to create a balance between enough time for their child and enough time for homework. Mothers compensated for a lack of information that they felt when comparing kindergarten and school, by interrogating their child, seeking more contact with the teacher and other parents. Thus they *adapted to different institutional norms*. While the children were in kindergarten there was an emphasis on autonomy but, in response to school entry, *relationships became traditionalised,* with parents having higher expectations regarding obedience and submission to demands from adults and to parental control.

Mothers were expected to adapt their working schedule to the needs of the child and her/his school's timetable. This is another aspect of traditionalisation of family roles.

Six months later most mothers granted more autonomy again to their children. This might have been the consequence of either resistance of the child or of feedback by the teacher.

With homework, parents (mothers) were eager to ensure their child performed well so as to reduce concern and anxiety, the latter being influenced by high aspirations. Mothers tried *to cope by over-fulfilling the task* (cf. Paetzold, 1988). Fathers in some cases reported messages to the child about the meaning of school performance for the child's future life that surely created achievement pressure.

Parents enjoyed their child's new competencies and felt pride in being the parent of a schoolchild. *Stressing the positive aspects* is important in coping with transition to school (cf. Kienig, 1999). When parents were asked to imagine the future, scepticism regarding the school's increasing demands was expressed. *Keeping some scepticism* can also be understood as a coping strategy as it works as a protection against lessening the efforts in uncompleted transitions. Coping with the transition to school was evidently a family activity.

Conclusion

Kindergarten in Germany in some aspects has a contradictory philosophy to school: social integration is a substantial function of kindergarten, while social selection is a substantial function of the school system (cf. Broström, 1999). What children and parents told us about their expectations also reflects this dichotomy. From this research we very clearly see a united as well as biographically unique experience for first-born children *and* parents. Both experience the transition as a process of co-construction (Dahlberg *et al.*, 1999). What parents expect, fear and hope, influences their child both through verbal and non-verbal messages, as well as through parental efforts to support their child. Reports that their own well-being and their way of dealing with the demands of their new familial situation depended on how well their child was doing in school, is one example of these reciprocal effects.

Although kindergarten as well as school teachers experience a very demanding time each year guiding children and parents during the transition into kindergarten and school, they do not have to cope with a comparably strong emotional arousal, nor do they develop a new identity. They do not experience the transition themselves but they can be regarded as contributors in the co-construction of the transition experience through their influence on children and parents. Parents and educators need to enter a dialogue about pedagogical concepts to prepare children for coping with the transition to school as preparation is needed not only for children, but also for parents. The family and the teacher can co-construct the transition processes through family socialisation in connection with educational institutions.

In a wider perspective, coping with transitions as well as developing resilience and competence in methods of learning will be basic competencies of members in a society characterised by discontinuities and change. They should be addressed within educational contexts in all settings: Family as well as kindergarten and school (Fthenakis, 2000).

References

Beelmann, W. (2001) 'Normative Übergänge im Kindesalter: eine differentielle Analyse des Anpassungsprozesses beim Eintritt in den Kindergarten, die Grundschule und die weiterführende Schule', Habilitationsschrift, University of Köln.

Berger, M. (1997) *Der Übergang von der Familie zum Kindergarten: Anregungen zur Gestaltung der Aufnahme in den kindergarten*, 2nd edn. Munich: E. Reinhardt.

Bronfenbrenner, U. (1979) *The Ecology of Human Development*. Cambridge, MA: Harvard University Press.

Broström, S. (1999) 'Educational contradictions between kindergarten and kindergarten classes in school in Denmark'. Paper presented at the 9th European Conference on Quality in Early Childhood Education 'Quality in Early Childhood Education – How Does Early Education Lead to Life-Long Learning?', Helsinki.

Cowan, P. (1991) 'Individual and family life transitions: a proposal for a new definition'. In P. Cowan and M. Hetherington (eds), *Family Transitions: Advances in Family Research*. Hillsdale, NJ: Lawrence Erlbaum.

Dahlberg, G., Moss, P. and Pence, A. (1999) *Beyond Quality in Early Childhood Education and Care: Postmodern Perspectives*. Philadelphia, PA: Falmer Press.

Dencik, L. (1997)'Modernization – a challenge to early childhood education. Scandinavian experiences and perspectives'. Keynote lecture given at 7th European Conference on the Quality of Early Childhood Education, Munich.

Fabian, H. (1998) 'Developing a conceptual framework for children's induction to the reception class and their transitions through school'. Paper presented at the 8th European Conference on the Quality of Early Childhood Education, Santiago de Compostela.

Filipp, S.-H. (1995) 'Ein allgemeines Modell für die Analyse kritischer Lebensereignisse', in S.-H. Filipp (ed.), *Kritische Lebensereignisse*, 3rd edn. Weinheim: Psychologie Verlags Union.

Fthenakis, W.E. (1998) 'Family transitions and quality in early childhood education', *European Early Childhood Education Research Journal* 6, 5–17.

Fthenakis, W.E. (2000) 'Konzeptionelle Neubestimmung von Bildungsqualität in Tageseinrichtungen für Kinder mit Blick auf den Übergang in die Grundschule – ein neuer Modellversuch im Staatsinstitut für Frühpädagogik', *Bildung, Erziehung, Betreuung von Kindern in Bayern* 5, 19.

Fuhs, B. (2000) 'Qualitative Interviews mit Kindern. Überlegungen zu einer schwierigen Methode'. In F. Heinzel (ed.), *Methoden der Kindheitsforschung. Ein Überblick über Forschungszugänge zur kindlichen Perspektive*. Weinheim/Munich: Juventa.

Griebel, W. and Niesel, R. (1997) 'From family to kindergarten: a common experience in a transition perspective'. Paper presented at 7th European Conference on the Quality of Early Childhood Education 'Childhood in a Changing Society', Munich.

Griebel, W. and Niesel, R. (1999) 'From kindergarten to school: a transition for the family'. Paper presented at the 9th European Conference on Quality in Early Childhood

Education 'Quality in Early Childhood Education – How Does Early Education Lead to Life-Long Learning?', Helsinki.

Griebel, W. and Niesel, R. (2000a) 'The children's voice in the complex transition into kindergarten and school'. Paper presented at the 10th European Conference on Quality in Early Childhood Education 'Complexity, Diversity, and Multiple Perspectives in Early Childhood Services', London.

Griebel, W. and Niesel, R. (2000b) 'Iz decjeg vrtica u skolu – prelazak za celu porodicu', *Norma* 1–2, 297–311.

Haefele, B. and Wolf-Filsinger, M. (1986) 'Der Kindergarten-Eintritt und seine Folgen – eine Pilotstudie', *Psychologie in Erziehung und Unterricht* 33, 99–107.

Heinzel, F. (2000) 'Kinder in Gruppendiskussionen und Kreisgesprächen'. In F. Heinzel (ed.), *Methoden der Kindheitsforschung. Ein Überblick über Forschungszugänge zur kindlichen Perspektive.* Weinheim/Munich: Juventa.

Hülst, D. (2000) 'Ist das wissenschaftlich kontrollierte Verstehen von Kindern möglich?'. In F. Heinzel (ed.), *Methoden der Kindheitsforschung. Ein Überblick über Forschungszugänge zur kindlichen Perspektive.* Weinheim/Munich: Juventa.

Kienig, A. (1998) 'Developmental disharmonies and pre-school setting adaptation of children', *International Journal of Early Years Education* 6, 143–53.

Kienig, A. (1999) 'Adjustment to new setting in the early years: how to help children in this transition'. Paper presented at the 9th European Conference on Quality in Early Childhood Education 'Quality in Early Childhood Education – How Does Early Education Lead to Life-Long Learning?', Helsinki.

Laewen, H.J. (1989) 'Nichtlineare Effekte einer Beteiligung von Eltern am Eingewöhnungsprozess von Kindergartenkindern. Die Qualität der Mutter–Kind-Bindung als vermittelnder Faktor', *Psychologie in Erziehung und Unterricht* 36, 102–8.

Lazarus, R.S. and Folkman, S. (1987) *Stress appraisal and coping.* New York: Springer.

Nickel, H. (1990) 'Das Problem der Einschulung aus ökologisch-systemischer Perspektive', *Psychologie in Erziehung und Unterricht* 37, 217–27.

Niesel, R. and Griebel, W. (2000) *Start in den kindergarten. Grundlagen und Hilfen zum Übergang von der Familie in die Kindertagesstätte.* München: Don Bosco.

Olbrich, E. (1995) 'Normative Übergänge im menschlichen Lebenslauf: Entwicklungskrisen oder Herausforderungen'. In S.-H. Filipp (ed.), *Kritische Lebensereignisse,* 3rd edn. Weinheim: Psychologie Verlags Union.

Paetzold, B. (1988) *Familie und Schulanfang. Eine Untersuchung des mütterlichen Erziehungsverhaltens.* Bad Heilbrunn: Klinkhardt.

Petzold, M. (1992) 'Die Einschulung des Kindes und die Erwartungen der Eltern – eine kleine Pilotstudie', *Zeitschrift für Familienforschung* 4, 160–70.

Pianta, R.C. (1999) 'Enhancing Relationships between Children and Teachers,, Washington, DC: American Psychological Association.

Scholz, G. (1994) *Die Konstruktion des Kindes.* Opladen: Westdeutscher Verlag.

Sirsch, U. (2000) *Psychologische Probleme beim Schulwechsel.* Münster: Waxmann.

van Gennep, A. (1960) *Rites of Passage.* London: Routledge and Kegan Paul.

Welzer, H. (1993) *Transitionen. Zur Sozialpsychologie biographischer Wandlungsprozesse.* Tübingen: Edition Discord.

Zinnecker, J. (1996) 'Grundschule als Lebenswelt des Kindes. Plädoyer für eine pädagogische Ethnographie'. In T. Bartmann and H. Ulonska (eds), *Kinder in der Grundschule. Anthropologische Grundlagenforschung.* Bad Heilbrunn: Klinkhardt.

Chapter 6

Parents' views of transition to school and their influence in this process

Inge Johansson

The transition from pre-school to school is a crucial period for a child. The first contact with the new setting in school is of vital importance for how the child will experience the school as an arena for learning and social development in the future. In this sense pre-school can be conceptualised as a setting that prepares the child and the parents for school.

The school system in Sweden has recently been reformed. Before the reform pre-schools were the responsibility of the Ministry of Social Affairs whilst school was, and continues to be, the responsibility of the Ministry of Education. Three significant changes brought by school reform in 1998 were:

- the introduction of new and related curriculum for each stage of education;
- that six-year-olds would be included in school, in pre-school classes; and
- that the recreation centre (*a pedagogical service that the parents can choose for their child to attend before and after the regular school-day, and attended by the majority*) should normally be connected to the school.

There are two main trends brought about by these changes: decentralisation and the widening role of the school. The first appears to bring about greater opportunities for parental influence whereas with the latter this is harder to judge. As a result, whilst the content of the school, used to mean what goes on inside the school and how that affects the child, is defined by the overall goals in the curriculum, in terms of decentralisation the content should also reflect the needs of the local area at the meso-level of local society (Bronfenbrenner, 1979; Bronfenbrenner and Vasta, 1989). This provides a strong incentive for increased influence from parents. Such influence can be broadly understood to include the power to influence change, in formal or informal ways. Secondly the role of the school has moved beyond that of the traditional school with its clear structure, limited by a strict time schedule and teaching physically located in the classroom, to include other aspects. This widened task involves a more global way of learning including stimulation of all children's senses and a combination of social and intellectual development. Considered from a perspective of social control this implies a tighter institutional social network in which the child is attached to the same group and the same pedagogues over a long period in a variety of situations and activities. This kind of control, for good or bad, is becoming strongly embedded in practice. This latter process is harder to judge in relation to parents' actual opportunities to be more active in school and to influence its content.

This implies that there could be a gap between rhetoric and reality. In our study we wanted to 'go behind' the vision and ask the parents themselves.

Background

The relation between school and its context is historically, culturally and socially formed in a tradition, a 'picture', of what school is about and what it represents in the public consciousness. The school in many western societies has a long tradition as an institution with its content defined by central government and its central institutions and not much interfered with by the local society. The school had its own rules and tasks which represented a system of punishment and exclusion for those who didn't want or could not adjust to it, as well as providing rewards for those who were successful. School and schooling had, and still have, a major role in how the society is formed, and in the extent to which it is integrated or segregated.

From this perspective school has been and still is a powerful institution. Power can mean different things. One is to have preferential right of interpretation. The teacher, as professional civil servant, is regarded as capable of interpreting what the child needs to develop and learn and, most importantly, what actions should be taken to realise this.

The new curriculum (Utbildningsdepartementet, 1998) states that this interpretation should be a common task for the teacher and the parents.

This implies that the power could be seen as a relation of exchange, that is the relationship between two participants could be mutual with both of them having power in relation to the other. Teachers are positive about parental collaboration if it is supportive to their work. The opposite can also be seen (Ravn, 1989). Viewed in this way two individuals or groups can be successful in using each other as resources to satisfy their own interests (Carleheden, 1996). Another concept often used is 'influence'. This is a more democratically oriented and less ideologically affected concept but one which is hard to define. The process of influence is often 'under the surface' and may only be seen in its manifestations: the intentions and actions are more loosely coupled than in relations based on power.

One of the main questions in this process is how to increase the power of the parents, how to strengthen their empowerment. One of the factors that has given more power to the parents is that they now in Sweden have the right to choose which school their child should go to.

In recent years the traditional relationships between teachers and parents have become more uncertain and contentious (Moore and Lasky, 1999). In a Canadian study the researchers conclude that parents have become more questioning and critical about issues of curriculum, the quality of instruction and practices used to assess and evaluate their children. The relationship between home and school are changing for a multitude of reasons, including greater diversity in parent population, changes in family structures, increasing school choice, more parental involvement in the governance of schools and new methods of local evaluation. These trends are significant in most countries, including Sweden.

Since parents are not a homogenous group, conflicts concerning expectations between parents and teachers, home and school culture and institutional barriers are bound to arise. Involving parents as real partners in the school requires an understanding of their aspirations for their children, their approach to parenting and their expectations of schooling including their perceptions of the pedagogues' roles and responsibilities. When parents are involved in the daily activities in the school and the services related to it, tensions may surface between professional and personal realities and preferences. For example when the parent feels the responsibility to fulfil their child's needs and the teacher at the same time feels a general responsibility to fulfil the needs for all the children in the group.

Results from our study (Johansson, 2000) and from other related research have shown that the support from the parents and how they regard the transition are highly influential on how the child adjusts to the new situation. In this project the parents' views of their children's transition and how they look upon the first period in school have been studied: some results are presented and discussed here. Two aspects that have an impact are the engagement of parents and whether or not they have made an active choice of school.

The context

In common with many schools in Sweden, the eight schools in this study incorporate pre-school class, school and recreational centre under the leadership of a head-teacher. Teams consisting of pre-school teachers, schoolteachers and recreational pedagogues share a joint responsibility for the content of the service informed by a local common goal document.

The study

We have studied how reformed school organisation has affected its content, especially the co-operation between the traditional school and the new service for six-year-olds (called the 'pre-school class') and also between school and the recreational centre. The eight schools chosen reflected the following criteria:

- a local documented common goal-document, for pre-school-class, school and recreational centre;
- teams consisting of pre-school teachers, schoolteachers and recreational pedagogues with a joint responsibility for the content of the service;
- a single headteacher for the combined service

We asked a sample group of 230 parents, representing 50 per cent of the six- or seven-year-old children in the sample schools at the beginning of 1999, about their view of this new situation, for their children and for themselves. To do this a questionnaire was developed containing questions about the following aspects.

The parents' knowledge of the new organisation in school, and their views about:

- the information given;
- the comfort and well-being of their child;
- the best and worst aspect of the current content in the service;
- the way that the current content affects the child's learning;
- the current way the staff works;
- their own general influence ;
- the service.

Most of the questions were formulated with fixed alternatives. Some also included the opportunity to add a written comment about how the parent looked upon the content and direction of the service.

The parents of six-year-olds and seven-year-olds were equally distributed. Also the distribution between girls and boys to parents in the response group were the same. For ethical reasons a control group methodology was not adopted, however the response rate of 132 out of the original 230, or two out of three, means that we have a fairly good representation from the goal group in our results. The response rate was fairly equally spread among the schools. The presentation of the results in the following tables includes, unless otherwise stated, the response from these 132 questionnaires.

Choice of school

As earlier mentioned it's now possible for the parents to choose to which school their child will go. All the services in our study, with two exceptions, lie in such socio-geographical areas that there is a realistic possibility for the parents to have a free choice of school for their children.

The majority of the parents answered however, that they *had not* made an active choice. We asked the minority of 61 parents who said they had made an active choice of a certain school about their reasons for so doing. The most frequently given reason was that the school had a 'good location', which normally means that it is in the neighbourhood (34 per cent of the parents said so). The second most frequent reason was that the content of the school was regarded as of good quality and especially its pedagogical profile. The rest of the parents said that the fact that the teachers of a certain school were skilled or that the child's friends all went to the same school had affected their choice.

In this respect there were clear differences between the schools. In two of them all the parents that took part in the study had actively chosen it. In two of the other schools none had made an active choice.

Knowledge about the school's organisation and attitude to information

The parents' knowledge of the main principles of how the new service in school is organised is generally very good. Nearly all of them know that the pedagogues collaborate in teams and that one headteacher leads the new integrated service. More than eight out of ten also knew that the school and the integrated service had common goals. A higher proportion of those who had actively chosen the school have this knowledge of the work in mixed teams and common goals, compared to the other parents. This implies that the active choice, which carries positive attitudes to the school has led to greater knowledge about the way of organising the integrated service.

The picture above is supported by the parents' answers about how they perceive the information given to them before their child started school. The majority say that they are fully satisfied with the information given. But it is also interesting to note that over one third say that they would like to have more information. Only a fraction of the parents answered that the information given to them has been completely insufficient.

The most satisfied in respect to the information given are parents with a six-year-old. This is interesting because those parents have children who have begun in a new service, namely the 'pre-school class'. The parents who have actively chosen the school report greater satisfaction than those who have not that they have completely sufficient information. This is also reasonable as it is to be expected that those who have been active in the choice are also more interested in the school and the matters there.

Comfort and well-being of the children

We asked how the parents viewed the comfort and well-being of their child in the service. Table 6.1 shows the number who has the opinion that their child is very well off in this respect in various parts of the integrated service. One group says that their child is comfortable in the recreational centre, pre-school class and school all together. Because of this the number of answers exceed the number of parents.

As we can see, the highest proportion is among the parents with a child in the pre-school class. The proportions of parents who believe the comfort and well–being of their child is high are fairly equal between school and recreational centre. Among those in the latter group there are also a handful saying that their child is

Table 6.1 The parents' opinion of the comfort and well-being of their child

Number of answers that comfort and well-being is very good	Percentage
Pre-school class (n = 68)	66
School (n = 80)	55
Recreational centre (n = 95)	58

not so well off: indeed the highest number of parents with this opinion is among those with their child in the recreational centre.

Parents who made an active choice of school are also the highest proportion of parents who are very satisfied with their children's well-being in school. This difference is largest for the group with their child in pre-school class. One difficulty in interpretation of such results is the well known influence from cognitive dissonance (Kiesler and Kiesler, 1970), which means that if one has already made an active choice, there is a tendency to stick to this and stress the positive aspect of the chosen matter, compared to the other alternatives. This means that there is a tendency that the parents from the 'active' group are more positive than they 'should' be.

We also asked the parents to describe in their own words what they think is the greatest advantage of the integrated service for their child. Among those who had their child in a pre-school class the response rate indicates the best aspect to be an appropriate combination of play and learning for the child. Other frequent categories were that the younger children had the opportunity to mix with the older ones in school, that being in a small group gave security and confidence for the child, and good staff was also an aspect mentioned. The principle of combining play and learning among the six-year-olds was stressed in a more positive way for boys compared to girls. For the girls the parents gave priority to security and to be in a small group.

Parents who had a child in the school answered the same question. The most frequently cited answer on the best thing about the school is that the children are stimulated there and that there are competent teachers guiding them. A further answer is about the quality of the peer relations for the child.

For the recreational centre the parents who answered this question say that the best thing is that the children can meet with peers there. Frequent mention is made of the continuity with school that staying at the service provides: the day becomes a whole unity for the children, and that the children get stimulation as well as the staff being good.

Overall, the answers from the parents show that they have a positive view of the integrated service in respect to the children's comfort and well-being there and also of its general content. Their descriptions match positively with the main aims of each service as formulated in documented goals on the local as well as the central level.

What functions best and worst?

Unlike the question presented above, which was directed towards how the parents perceived the content of the service for their child, two more generally formulated questions were asked concerning what the parents saw as the best and the worst aspect of the integrated service as a whole.

Many parents emphasise the aspects providing continuity and integration. This indicates that the parents share the main principles for the organisation of the new services. Many also stress the competence of staff as a main quality. In this respect there are no differences due to active choice of school or not.

When asked about the worst aspect of the integrated service the parents mainly stressed three things. As can be expected the most frequent answer is that there are too few grown-ups and too many children in each group. The second aspect describes that the after-school service was insufficiently planned and the physical facilities and the environment, on the whole, were insufficient. The poor rating of these aspects are related to the notion that there are too few employees and too many children in the groups.

Whilst the parents of girls tend to be more dissatisfied with the above-mentioned structure of the group, among the parents of boys there is a predominant dissatisfaction with the physical facilities and the environment.

Influence on learning

The parents were asked their view of how the new way of working in the integrated service influenced the children's learning. This question was put to the parents in an open way, meaning that we did not define the concept of learning to the parents. Their answers are shown in Table 6.2.

Most of the six-year-olds come from pre-schools. As the services in our study have been running for more than a year it is most likely that the seven-year-olds previously have attended a pre-school class connected to school. The majority says that the children learn more in the new situation than they did before. These results, though, would be best interpreted in the light of the parents' own frames of reference for making such a judgement, these are, however, unknown to us.

Parents of boys especially stress that they learn more now than before. In spite of the bias of interpretation the parents' opinion appears as a good judgement of the content of the integrated service and its effect on children's learning. This tendency is especially strong among parents of seven-year-olds, which means children that have just begun school. This indicates that the school-start is a marked transition from one form of service to another, but not necessarily a problematic one.

Quality in the new service and the way it works

The parents were asked to respond to some positive features that were likely to be found in the integrated service. They could respond to more than one. The percentages in Table 6.3 could therefore not be summarised to 'one hundred'. Results are ranked in their presentation.

Parents stressed the qualities of the grown-ups' competence and the relationships between them and the children. Most important, according to the parents, is that the children have access to a group of grown-ups who differ in their skills and with whom the children can relate.

Table 6.2 What does the new way of working mean for children's learning?

What the new way of working means for children's learning	Percentage (n = 96)
The children learn more now than before	62
The children learn as much as before, there is no difference	32
The children learn less than before	6

Table 6.3 The greatest advantage of the current way of working

What is best thing about the current way of working?	Percent (n = 132)
There are groups of grown-ups with a varied competence who are available to support the children	77
The children meet the same staff during the whole day	60
More grown-ups available so that the child always has someone to relate to	59
The children have better possibilities to learn at their own pace	54
The situation means that the children can feel secure	49
The children receive stimulation adapted to their personal needs	37

The content of the service, as the parents see it, is group-oriented. Few parents feel that the child receives stimulation adapted to individual needs. Parents of the youngest children, six-year-olds, stress security the most. The quality most stressed by parents of the school children is that they have better possibilities to learn at their own speed. These results suggest that the parents generally have a positive opinion that the school can satisfy the children's need to learn at their own speed on a surface level, but that the individual needs of each child on a deeper level are satisfied to a far lesser extent.

What is problematic?

In a similar way to the earlier question the parents were asked about aspects they would describe as problematic in the service. The most problematic thing for parents is that the group of children is large. Parents also mentioned that it can be difficult to recognise what the children learn and that the organisation of the service could be messy. Not so many agree with the statements that their child had too little contact with grown-ups and that there is a risk of the pre-school class becoming too much like 'school' for the six-year-olds.

There are no significant differences between how the parents who have made an active choice of school answer in relation to the others. There is a tendency that the 'active' parents are more critical of the large groups of children in the service, that it is poorly organised there, and the children are left too much on their own, compared to the other group of parents.

The parents' influence on the content of the school

This part consisted of three questions. One was about how influence from parents generally could be seen; one was about the view of one's own influence, and the third reflected how one perceived the change in influence during the last year.

Approximately three out of four parents who answered the first question said that parent's influence was sufficient in the current situation. The rest had the opinion that parents had too little influence.

The same tendency could be seen when the parents answered the question about how they perceived their own influence. The majority was generally satisfied with their current influence. Out of the 124 who answered this question 69 per cent said that their influence was good enough and that they were satisfied with it. Among the rest 25 per cent wanted more influence and a small group responded that they had no interest in influencing the content of the school as this was mainly a matter for the professional staff.

The majority could not see any particular change in influence during the last year. One out of three (36 per cent) said that the parental influence had increased lately. Just two persons said the influence had declined during the last year.

Those who made an active choice of school were generally more satisfied with their influence compared to the 'less active'. Among the 'active' group there is also a comparatively high proportion that would like to increase their influence.

This indicates that an active choice of school also includes a wish for strong influence on the service. There is also among parents in the 'active' group the opinion that the influence has increased significantly. To have a significant influence leads to more influence.

On the whole these results show a generally positive picture of how parents perceive their influence on the integrated service. The most important factor in this respect is whether the parents have made an active choice of school or not. This is more important than the child's age and gender.

Discussion

As the results indicate the parents in our study have a generally good knowledge of, and influence upon, the new integrated service, especially among the group that have made an active choice of school for their child. The parents see the new way of working together and co-operating in the integrated service as good quality. An example of this is the perception that the children learn more in the new service than they have done previously.

Another indication of good quality is that the opinions of both parents and staff have a high degree of correspondence. For example, both groups stress highly the importance of there being more than one adult in the setting so the children can develop various contacts with adults in order to better fulfil their needs. Parents and staff also share the opinion that the biggest problem is that there are too few adults and too many children in each group. This kind of agreement and shared views of the same context could be seen as a quality in itself (Johansson, 1999) and create a good climate for a further development of influence from parents.

To be active is a process. Our results show that an active choice of school also implies an active relationship to its content. But activity is also a matter of resources. In our study we did not have any data on the resources, manifest or latent among the parents. Institutions are connected to power; they often represent civic power in themselves. In this sense power is also represented by the professions and the staff in these institutions. The crucial question is how the parents are 'invited' into the institutions and how they are empowered to relate to them. It would be naive to expect educators and school boards to simply hand over institutional-based power to parents (Moore and Lasky, 1999). The challenge for educators and parents is to find ways to work collaboratively on the basis of each other's practice, in the best interest of the child's learning and development. We need to find and analyse good examples of such collaboration in the future and be able to learn from them in a practical way.

The process of increasing the parents' influence and their collaboration in the new integrated services is about two main things, democratisation on the one hand and professionalisation on the other. The way in which these aspects are connected to each other is of great importance. In a Finnish study, many teachers thought that the real power was on the political and administrative level (Nuutinen, 1999). Parents were rated more positively than politicians and administrators. In the future one way to develop parents' influence is for the professionals to collaborate with them to strengthen the status and level of resources given to the local school.

Some structural aspects also prevent parents from being critical and in this way create a dialogue with teachers. The risk of hurting a teacher's feelings can prevent parents from engaging in an 'honest' discussion with teachers, even if they are able to present good evidence for their criticism. Put simply, they are anxious for what would happen to their children. Who would like to take such a risk? That is why it is so important to establish a relation between the professionals and parents that rests on confidence and trust.

The most important factor that prevents parents from taking a more active part in their children's service is time (Ståhle, 2000). This prompts questions for the whole of society: how to handle time-based choices and constraints and what priorities are made on a more global level to give children a space in life. Other results from research indicate that parents' active support in their child's transition from pre-school to school affects their child's first time in school in a highly positive way. Most of such positive influence can be related to parents' feelings of security, involvement and being invited to take part in the transition process. This affects the child and the whole important emotional situation during the transition in a positive way. We have found a significant positive connection between support from parents and how easy that transition to school had been (Johansson, 1995).

In the future, critical analyses must be made concerning the parents actual needs for influence and ways to develop it on the one hand and political manifestations and central ideology on the other hand.

References

Bronfenbrenner, U. (1979) *The Ecology of Human Development*. Cambridge, MA: Harvard University Press.

Bronfenbrenner, U. and Vasta, R. (1989) 'Ecological systems theory'. In Bronfenbrenner, U. and Vasta, R. (eds), *Annuals of Child Development. Six Theories of Child Development: Revised Formulations and Current Theories*. London: JAI Press.

Carleheden, M. (1996) *Det andra moderna. Om Jurgen Habermas och den samhälls-teoretiska diskursen om det moderna (That Other Modern. About Jürgen Habermas and the Discourse of Societal Theory)*. Göteborg: Daidalos.

Johansson, I. (1995) 'New services for six-year-olds in Stockholm. Content and directions', *European Early Childhood Educational Research Journal* 3(1).

Johansson, I. (1999) *Samarbete, effektivitet, kvalitet i integrerade verksamheter för sexåringar, skola och fritidshem (Collaboration, Efficiency, Quality in Integrated Services for Six-year-olds, School and Recreational Centre)*. FoU-rapport 1999: 5. Stockholm: FoU-enheten.

Johansson, I. (2000) *Innehållet i den nya skolan. (The Content of the New School)*. FoU-rapport 2000: 8. Stockholm: FoU-enheten.

Kiesler, C. and Kiesler S. (1970) *Conformity*. London: Addison-Wesley Publishing Company.

Nuutinen, P. (1999) 'Being power partners'. In Smit, F., Moerlel, H., Van der Wolf, K. and Sleegers, P. (eds), *Building Bridges Between Home and School*. Nijmegen: Institute for Applied Social Sciences. University of Nijmegen.

Moore, S. and Lasky, S. (1999) 'Parent involvement in education: models, strategies and contexts'. In Smit, F., Moerlel, H., Van der Wolf, K. and Sleegers, P. (eds), *Building Bridges Between Home and School*. Nijmegen: Institute for Applied Social Sciences. University of Nijmegen.

Ravn, B. (1989) *Myter, Magt of Muligheter (Myths, Power and Possibilities)*. Vejle: Kroghs forlag.

Ståhle, Y. (2000): *Föräldrainflytande i skolan, behov eller politisk viljeyttring? (Parents Influence in School, Actual Need or Political Manifestation?)* FoU-rapport 2000: 2. Stockholm: FoU-enheten.

Utbildningsdepartementet (The Swedish Ministry of Education) (1998) *Läroplan för det obligatoriska skolväsendet, förskoleklassen och fritidshemmet. (Curriculum for the Compulsory School, Pre-school Class and the Recreational Center)*. Stockholm: Utbildningsdepartementet.

Chapter 7

Teachers' perspectives of transition

Sally Peters

This chapter discusses early childhood and school teachers' perspectives on the transition to school. While children, their families and their teachers are all key players in the transition process, teachers hold the ultimate power in the classroom (Jackson, 1987). Therefore, the responsibility for many of the recommendations discussed in other chapters regarding ways in which transition can be enhanced inevitably rests with teachers. However, as child–school incorporation is a dynamic and interactive process between all the participants (Ghaye and Pascal, 1988), the teachers' role cannot be seen in isolation. Looking at ways in which teachers can facilitate transition needs to take into account the teachers' own perspectives, and the ways in which these are influenced.

Drawing on the work of Vygotsky, Graue (1993) discusses how meanings are negotiated socially and then internalised by individuals. She found that teachers' perspectives and practices differed in different school settings and both shaped and were shaped by the views of parents, teaching colleagues and others. Teachers' ideas are also influenced by school philosophy and organisation (Smith and Shepherd, 1988). Wider sources of influence are also evident. For example, in recent years national curricula and assessment practices have led to pressure to 'push down' the primary school curriculum into early childhood (Carr, 2001; Corrie, 1999; May, 2000). Also, what happens in practice is likely to be dependent, not only on teacher beliefs and influences, but also moderated by a range of contextual factors (Bennett *et al.*, 1997). Exploring the complexity of these issues is an important step in developing policies and practices that enhance the transition experiences of children and their families.

Research approach

The overall study from which the data in this chapter are drawn explored the experiences of twenty-three children, their families and their teachers during the children's transition to school. A qualitative approach was used and data were gathered by means of interviews and detailed observations in early childhood services and new entrant classrooms, and collection of relevant documentation. The main data collection period was within a single school year. However, for seven of the twenty-three children and their families data collection began during the children's last term at kindergarten and continued until they had been at school for three years. The findings presented here draw mainly from teacher interviews and observations during the initial twelve months of the study. An interpretive methodology has been used to identify and analyse the concepts, relationships and issues within a detailed case study design (Graue and Walsh, 1998). Pseudonyms have been used for the name of the school, the kindergartens and the participants.

The research settings and participating teachers

The research settings were Kowhai School, an urban primary school with a roll of about 500 pupils and three contributing kindergartens. The three kindergartens were the main early childhood services used by the seven case study children.

At Kowhai School the new entrant teachers, Ms Keane, Ms King and Ms Knight had between twelve and twenty years experience of primary school teaching, with at least three at the new entrant level. The Assistant Principal had over thirty years teaching experience.

One of the three teachers in each kindergarten was interviewed. Ms Ashby (Azure Kindergarten), Ms Bird (Blue Kindergarten) and Ms Clarke (Cobalt Kindergarten), had between fifteen and eighteen years experience of teaching at the early childhood level. All nine kindergarten teachers were included in the observations.

Teachers' perspective on facilitating transition

The main theme that was evident in the teachers' views about transition related to issues of continuity between early childhood and school, both in children's learning and through transition visits and other forms of contact.

Teachers' perspectives on continuity in early learning

Azure Kindergarten was the only early childhood service that had any direct contact with Kowhai School. Over the years the school and kindergarten teachers had developed a close, respectful relationship. They tried to provide some continuity through similarities in the programmes at kindergarten and school (in terms of mat times, behaviour management techniques and language used). At kindergarten the teachers aimed to foster sets of dispositions or habitus (Carr, 2001), that both parties believed would allow children to participate effectively in the school environment. Ms Ashby's view was that early childhood education was a preparation for life, but she also felt that:

> ... school happens to be the next rung of the ladder of life and it is stupid to say that you are not preparing them for school because you are ... Some of

the things that we try to do particularly here is to develop their inquisitiveness and independence and self esteem ... They have also learnt to listen, to participate, to be part of a group and to respect people. They have got to learn to share ... To build the child's self esteem and to teach them independence and to encourage their inquiring mind so that they want to learn, want to find out about things.

Interestingly, although the new entrant teachers and many parents valued the preparation provided by Azure's programme, some parents believed that a more formal approach to teaching literacy and numeracy would provide 'a stepping stone to school'. Many of these parents were paying for their children to attend a private centre where this was offered. The attractive five-page brochure from the private centre claimed to provide four-year-olds with a programme that included writing their names, counting to ten, exploring the alphabet and print and following instructions 'so their transition from Kindy to School will be as easy as possible'. While similar skills were also developed at the state kindergartens, the emphasis and approach to teaching was different. Ms Ashby acknowledged that she tried to explain their approach to parents but it was sometimes difficult to compete with the private centre's marketing.

Parental pressure for a more school-like level of formality was even more evident at Blue Kindergarten. Ms Bird said she actively resisted this pressure, believing that discontinuity between the practices in the two settings did not have to be overcome by making the early childhood programme more formal. 'That's just a fact of life that the rules are different for different times and places in your life. We try very hard to tell them [parents] that it's not how we work with children. That we are not all going to sit and cut a circle because you have to do it type of thing'.

In practice, the children's actual experiences of transition suggested that the reasons why a child's transition was smooth or difficult went beyond simple explanations such a slight differences in the early childhood programme they had experienced (see Peters, 2000a). However, in responding to parental pressure, Ms Ashby's close relationship with the new entrant teachers meant that she was able to explain confidently how she believed that Azure's focus on certain dispositions would benefit children when they arrived at school. In contrast, Ms Bird, who had no direct contact with any schools, was less confident in her responses because she was unsure what actually happened in a new entrant classroom. 'What's happening now is different to when my children went'. Ms Bird felt it would be useful to establish contact with some of the local schools, including Kowhai. She said: 'I am sure that they don't know what we do here and we don't know what they do there and it seems like there is this huge gap ... I think we need to know what each other is doing'.

At Cobalt Kindergarten, which was some distance from the other two, and only occasionally fed into Kowhai School, the teachers were not aware of any pressure from parents to introduce a more formal approach. Ms Clark's perspective on continuity was that children should be prepared 'for life' rather than for school, but she did try to foster the skills that she thought would 'make the transition easier'. These included:

> Being able to identify their name, knowing how to look after their belongings and where they go. Self help skills would be the first ones ... I'm not too worried about writing names... when children are ready they will do that ... Knowing how to hold a pencil ... Socialisation, knowing how to ask for help if you need it ... I see it more a holistic, all round thing.
>
> (Ms Clark)

The skills the school teachers said that they thought were useful to have on entry to school were broadly similar to those mentioned by Ms Ashby and Ms Clarke. These included independence in learning and in practical skills such as dressing, eating and using the toilet, and the ability to listen, to sit still and take turns. Their views are consistent with the findings of a much larger survey of 217 Australian teachers (Perry *et al.*, 2000). The new entrant teachers also said they valued social skills, the ability to stay on task, to be able to hold a pencil and scissors, and to use materials like paint and glue. They valued early childhood experiences that had helped to foster the skills they felt were helpful, and they took steps to provide some continuity between school and children's earlier experiences.

The school teachers differed in their individual requirements regarding academic skills, but overall there was a general sense that they could assess and build on children's existing knowledge, and that skills like reading and knowing numbers were not necessary on entry to school:

> That doesn't worry us particularly... we can help them with those things.
>
> (Assistant Principal)

> I would like them [early childhood teachers] to contribute more to the social and physical, emotional well-being of the child, that's the most crucial areas... the most academic thing that I really like them to be doing is to stay on task. To be able to work for five or ten minutes on a task.
>
> (Ms Knight)

In fact, with the exception of Ms King, they felt that some parents were overly concerned about children's academic performance. From the interview data therefore we might conclude that parents who were pressing for a more formal approach in early childhood were perhaps, like the children Broström describes in Chapter 4, operating from an outdated view of schooling. However, Graue (1993) highlights how meanings of readiness for school are constructed in communities, and the nature of what actually happened in the school programme may have helped to shape these parents' views.

The observations indicated that while there were elements of child-centred approaches and teacher-led activities in both settings, the move from kindergarten to school was characterised by a shift in the balance of these elements, from occasional teacher-led activities such as mat times at kindergarten, to a largely teacher-led programme at school. A large proportion of the tasks in the new entrant classroom seem likely to foster performance goals, rather than learning goals (utilising the descriptions of these provided by Carr (2001)). Many children found these tasks appropriately challenging and enjoyed their subsequent mastery of them, but for a few the focus on 'getting everything right' was disconcerting (see Peters, 2000a).

Although the new entrant teachers claimed that academic skills were not important on entry to school, in practice they appeared to have in mind a baseline level of competence, especially in letter recognition, reading and writing. Children who fell behind this line were quickly identified and their parents informed. Although such information was well meaning it caused anxiety in some families. At the same time the skills the new entrant teachers said they wanted children to have on entry to school such as independence and self-care skills were very important in the school environment, where a large group of five-year-old children spent the day with one adult. Social skills also proved to be very helpful (see Peters, 2000b). Teachers did not value academic ability above other skills like independence, but the nature of the assessment that was shared with parents/caregivers meant that literacy skills gained particular significance.

New entrant teachers were therefore providing somewhat mixed messages, valuing a fairly holistic approach to children's learning, but also providing a programme that included a number of formal elements and utilised skills-based assessments. As will be discussed later, these conflicting messages can be better understood by examining the complexity of the new entrant teacher's role, which is not just to foster learning but also to support children's adaptation to the school environment. However, it is perhaps not surprisingly that a number of parents responded by seeking more formal approaches in early childhood as preparation for school. Interestingly, close contact with the school actually helped Ms Ashby resist some of this pressure, while at Cobalt, where most of the children fed into a different primary school, there was no apparent pressure for more formality.

Close links between school and early childhood services formed the basis of the other key issue of continuity, which related to transition visits and other forms of contact.

Teachers' perspectives on transition visits and other forms of contact

The early childhood and new entrant teachers all believed that school visits were an important part of the transition process, although there were some differences regarding what they thought the nature and number of appropriate visits should be. At Kowhai School pre-entry visits were usually arranged from 9.00–10.30 on a morning near to when a child was due to turn five (based on the New Zealand practice of children starting school on their fifth birthday). This policy had been developed in conjunction with Azure Kindergarten and the kindergarten teachers took turns in taking small groups of children to visit their new entrant classrooms. On the day of the school visit the new entrant teachers and school principal would come to the Azure Kindergarten at lunchtime to meet with the children and their families and tell the parents/caregivers about school. The teachers in both settings felt that this arrangement worked very well.

There were no direct links between Kowhai School and any of the other contributing early childhood services, so for the children who did not attend Azure Kindergarten the parents/caregivers arranged a date with the new entrant teacher for the child's visit. These parents/caregivers did not have the opportunity to meet the school personnel in the way the parents/caregivers at Azure did at the lunchtime meeting, and were discouraged from staying during the child's visit, 'Because the children who are clingy can't cling to mum if she is not there and they will actually fit in quicker' (Ms King).

The teachers at all three kindergartens felt that having early childhood teachers take children for a school visit was beneficial because it gave the child a familiar adult as a support in the new environment. It also helped to foster links between the early childhood and the school settings. However, in a busy urban environment these visits were proving increasingly difficult, due to the large number of schools each early childhood service fed into and the large number of early childhood services that fed into each school. The situation at both Blue and Cobalt kindergartens was summed up by Ms Bird, who acknowledged 'the problem is we feed into so many schools. If you do it with one should you do it with all? Realistically that's not on'.

Although not able to visit with children themselves, Ms Bird and Ms Clarke had strong views about different schools' transition policies.

> From where I see it, it would be beneficial, especially for some children, to have anything up to four or more visits so that they are familiar with the classroom, the teacher and the layout … One or two [parents] are not happy with the current process and I generally grit my teeth and am not happy either … A couple of the local schools only allow one visit to maybe two or three and often it is only for an hour which I have a bit of a gripe about because I don't think an hour is particularly valid at all … Some of the feedback I get is that it has been quite traumatic for the child. Whether that has been the class environment or because the parent has been asked to leave, or the routine is quite different.
>
> (Ms Bird)

> Some are far more lenient than others and they [children] can go along five to six weeks beforehand. Some they are allowed only one session, they [the new entrant teachers] like the parent to disappear. They are different. Often we get

asked for our comments on that, and we just stay very, very, neutral ... Hopefully by the time the child is ready to start they will have done two to three visits.

(Ms Clarke)

Teachers in these two kindergartens saw their role in terms of ensuring parents had selected a school for their child and encouraging the parents to be proactive in requesting school visits. As Ms Bird stated 'I really encourage them to ask not "Can I?" but "I am going to bring the child for a visit, what day is appropriate?"' (p8). She would then follow up with the parent to find out how the visit had gone.

The gentle encouragement from the teachers at Blue and Cobalt kindergartens did seem to play a key role in empowering parents to request visits and to obtain modifications to the policy of one unaccompanied visit, to better meet the needs of their child. In comparison, the close kindergarten–school relationship and the well-established routine of visits at Azure Kindergarten, while having a number of advantages, worked in some cases to exclude parents. It also discouraged parents who felt that one school visit was insufficient from trying to obtain more, because the kindergarten teachers at Azure reinforced the message of 'only one school visit'.

Since the data were collected, many New Zealand kindergarten teachers have been prevented by their governing bodies from taking children on school visits. A number of reasons underpin this decision and there are local variations. This has placed the onus on parents to arrange visits for their children. The findings of this study suggest early childhood teachers have a vital role in encouraging and supporting parents during the process of selecting a school and arranging pre-entry visits. At the same time the perspectives of the new entrant teachers need to be kept in mind. The New Zealand practice of children starting school on their fifth birthday means that new entrant classes grow in size throughout the year and teachers have to balance the orientation of new children and their families with teaching an established group of children. At Kowhai School each of the three new entrant teachers oversaw the transition of about thirty children in the year of the study. With class sizes of up to twenty-nine, a large number of frequently visiting four-year-olds and their caregivers present more logistical difficulties than a single unaccompanied visit for each child, and may be more disruptive to the classroom process than they would be in a school where the overall class sizes were smaller or new children started less frequently. As opportunities for both children and families to have plenty of contact with schools prior to entry does seem to facilitate the transition process it is important to look at ways of making this manageable for the new entrant teacher.

At the same time, other forms of contact can be established. The kindergarten teachers felt it was useful for schools to provide information (school prospectuses, newsletters, etc.), that could be made available to parents/caregivers at the early childhood centre. Another idea, developed since the data were collected, has been for early childhood teachers to create display boards with photographs of new entrant classrooms and their teachers. Parents/caregivers can add their child's name or photo beneath the picture of the class the child is going to enter. This provides a forum for children to talk about who else will be in their class and to discuss some features of the school environment. Ms Clarke also believed it was important to talk to children about what might happen at school, 'So that you can actually correct them if they have got it wrong ... If they have been threatened 'You will be sitting on the mat all day' you can actually help them to realise what it will be like'. Fabian's stories and cartoons that focus on common school scenarios, discussed in Chapter 10, would fit well here.

As noted earlier, Ms Bird felt that occasional visits for early childhood teachers to new entrant classrooms, and for new entrant teachers to early childhood services, would be another useful step in facilitating transition. In addition, Ms Bird and Ms Clarke both hoped to host sessions where staff from a number of schools could meet with kindergarten teachers and parents/caregivers to facilitate communication between the different groups involved in transition. Although both suggestions require time and effort on the part of teachers at both levels in order to be successful, improved communication would seem to be a useful step in enhancing transitions. Combined professional development opportunities would provide another forum to support communication between early childhood and school teachers.

Final comments

Consideration of teachers' perspectives of transition serve to highlight some of the pedagogical issues in early years education and the tensions teachers face in meeting the competing demands of their role. One of the key pedagogical issues that arose for early childhood teachers was balancing their beliefs about appropriate education for young children with external pressure for a more formal approach. Corrie (1999) documents similar pressures in the UK, USA and Australia.

Responding to pressure for a more formal approach in early childhood

There are two important points that can be considered in relation to pressure for more formal approaches in early childhood. First, there is considerable evidence to suggest that the push down of formal approaches to teaching in early childhood is detrimental to children's learning in the long term (Blakemore, 2000; Elkind, 1987; Katz, 1993) and therefore it would disadvantage children to create continuity in this way. In this situation a distinctive early childhood curriculum and pedagogy can be seen as a positive (May, 2000). At the same time, early childhood teachers need to ensure that they are providing appropriate levels of challenge for children, and that they can articulate the learning that is taking place. As Elkind (1987) pointed out, parents [and others] cannot be blamed for valuing a more formal approach if what is valued as appropriate learning in early childhood is not explained clearly. Carr's (2001) learning story model of assessment, which looks at the following domains of children's learning dispositions; taking an interest, becoming involved, persisting with difficulty or uncertainty, communication with others, and taking responsibility, is likely to assist in both processes.

Second, while the New Zealand school curriculum framework is more skill and subject based than the early childhood curriculum, there is nothing in the school curriculum documents to indicate that a more formal approach is required in meeting the curriculum objectives, even at the school level. Yates (2001) maintains that 'schools today aspire to develop students who are independent thinkers and learners' (p145) and recent literature for primary schools describes a holistic, child-centred approach to children's learning (Fraser, 2001). Such an approach is consistent with early childhood philosophy and negates the need for a push down of formal approaches, which seem to belong to an earlier period in time and do not reflect current views of learning (see Barker, 2001). Therefore more persuasive arguments can be advanced for maintaining continuity through a continued focus on children's learning, across the transition period and beyond, rather than adopting a formal approach in early childhood.

However, arguments against a formal approach in early childhood may not convince parents unless they see these ideas reflected in their child's new entrant classroom. In this study child-centred approaches were clearly evident in the new entrant teachers' descriptions of some of the aspects they valued in children's learning, but these views sometimes contrasted with what happened in practice. These conflicting messages can be better understood by examining the complexity of the new entrant teacher's role, which is not just to foster learning but also to support children's adaptation to the school environment.

Understanding the complexity of the new entrant teacher's role

Parents in this study who were seeking more formal approaches in early childhood with a view to enhancing their children's learning would have been interested in Ms Knight's comment that she deliberately ensured they had 'quite a bit of formal stuff interjected through the day' because she believed that new entrant children enjoyed formal lessons, even though she acknowledged 'most of the learning doesn't happen that way'. Class size is probably a feature here, as it is with aspects of formality that relate to procedures and routines, which Cullen and St George (1996) found dominated in the new entrant classroom.

School entry policies are also influential. Yates (2001) notes that even with child-centred approaches the teacher needs to provide a framework for behaviour and therefore for learning. These rules and procedures would normally be established early in the school year, but when new children are continually joining the class such frameworks have to be revisited time and time again, which may lead to a focus on procedures rather than learning.

Cullen and St George (1996) observed a shift to a greater orientation to learning in the second year of school. However, this may be problematic unless an appropriate balance is found during the transition period. If children become too focused on performance goals in their new entrant year they may find it difficult to negotiate the move [back] to a learning goal orientation. A change in assessment practices might help to maintain a focus on children's learning throughout the transition period. Carr's (2001) work on learning stories as a framework for assessment could therefore also have important implications at the school level as well as in early childhood.

Conclusion

The teachers' perspectives of transition discussed in this chapter reveal the complexity of the topic. Teachers' views of their roles in facilitating the transition to school vary both within and across the early childhood and school sectors. Exploring these views helps to show how the teachers' perspectives are shaped by a number of other issues. For early childhood teachers much of the complexity seemed to come from competing views about appropriate early education, which could result in external pressure from parents and others. New entrant teachers seemed to face less external pressure in relation to their pedagogy but experienced internal tensions from the competing demands of their role, as they tried to balance espoused child-centred approaches to learning with the practicalities of helping up to thirty just-turned five-year-olds adapt to the rules and routines of the school environment. These demands also impacted on policies for transition visits and other forms of contact, as did current enrolment patterns and the mobility of families, which are creating an increasingly complex web of connections between early childhood services and schools. Understanding this complexity is an important aspect in the development of any policies and practices that seek to enhance the experiences of children and their families during the transition to school.

References

Barker, M. (2001) 'How do people learn? Understanding the learning process'. In C. McGee and D. Fraser (eds), *The Professional Practice of Teaching*, 2nd edn. Palmerston North: Dunmore Press.

Bennett, N., Wood, L. and Rogers, S. (1997) *Teaching Through Play*. Buckingham: Open University Press.

Blakemore, S.-J. (2000) *Early Years Learning POST 140*. London: The Parliamentary Office of Science and Technology.

Carr, M. (2001) *Assessment in Early Childhood Settings*. London: Paul Chapman.

Corrie, L. (1999) 'Politics, the provision of physical amenities, and the 'push-down' curriculum', *Australian Journal of Early Childhood* 24(3), 5–10.

Cullen, J. and St George, A. (1996) 'Scripts for learning: reflecting dynamics of classroom life', *Journal for Australian Research in Early Childhood Education* 1, 10–19.

Elkind, D. (1987) 'Superbaby syndrome can lead to elementary school burnout', *Young Children*, March, p. 14.

Fraser, D. (2001) 'Developing classroom culture: Setting the climate for learning'. In C. McGee and D. Fraser (eds), *The Professional Practice of Teaching*, 2nd edn. Palmerston North: Dunmore Press.

Ghaye, A. and Pascal, C. (1988) 'Four-year-old children in reception classrooms: participant perceptions and practice', *Educational Studies* 14(2), 187–208.

Graue, M.E. (1993) *Ready for What? Constructing Meanings of Readiness for Kindergarten*. New York: State University of New York Press.

Graue, M. and Walsh, D.J. (1998) *Studying Children in Context: Theories, Methods and Ethics*. London: Sage publications.

Jackson, M. (1987) 'Making sense of school'. In A. Pollard (ed.), *Children and Their Primary Schools: A New Perspective*. New York: Falmer Press.

Katz, L.G. (1993) *Dispositions: Definitions and Implications for Early Childhood Practices*. Perspectives from ERIC/EECE: A Monograph Series, No. 4. Urbana, IL: ERIC Clearinghouse on Elementary and Early Childhood Education.

May, H. (2000) 'Mapping the landscape of "the century of the child"', *New Zealand Annual Review of Education* 9, 117–32.

Perry, B., Dockett, S. and Howard, P. (2000) 'Starting school: issues for children, parents and teachers', *Journal of Australian Research in Early Childhood Education* 7, 41–53.

Peters, S. (2000a) 'Multiple Perspectives on Continuity in Early Learning and the Transition to School'. Paper presented at 'Complexity, diversity and multiple perspectives in early childhood', 10th European Early Childhood Education Research Association Conference, London.

Peters, S. (2000b) '"I didn't expect that I would get tons of friends ... more each day": children's experiences of friendship during the transition to school'. Paper presented at 'Surviving paradox: education in the new millennium'. NZARE Annual Conference, University of Waikato.

Smith, M.L. and Shepherd, L.A. (1988) 'Kindergarten readiness and retention: a qualitative study of teachers' beliefs and practices', *American Educational Research Journal* 25, 301–33.

Yates, R. (2001) 'Managing the learning environment'. In C. McGee and D. Fraser (eds), *The Professional Practice of Teaching*, 2nd edn. Palmerston North: Dunmore Press.

Chapter 8

Perspectives on children as learners in the transition to school

Aline-Wendy Dunlop

It is widely accepted that the passage through major changes in our lives can have lasting effects on how we see ourselves, the value we feel others place on us, our sense of well-being and consequently how we are able to learn. One of the major differences that occurs as children move from home to pre-school to school education is likely to be the way in which they are seen as learners. Different views of children as learners, including the children's own, may shed some light on why some children find such transitions easier than others. Children's ability to claim the new setting as their own and to benefit educationally from it, may be reflected in the degree to which their educators have collaborated in a shared conceptual framework of children's learning. This chapter considers what children are like as learners and whether or not parents', pre-school and primary educators' views of children differ.

This chapter draws on a study of continuity and progression in transition from pre-school settings to early primary education, in which fifteen pilot study children and twenty-eight main study children were tracked through pre-school and into their primary education. The likely impact of policy, cultural constructions of childhood, ideologies, psychological models and research on the children's experience is used as a vehicle to reflect on the origins of different views of children as learners and the conditions that consequently are created for that learning. The effects of differing views of children at school entry are addressed, including the views of children themselves.

Ideologies of early education

How society or the state views its children will determine what it provides, and thus externally constructed views of childhood may be planted onto existing services. For appropriate political decisions to be made, we need to be able to describe, analyse and share the pre-school and early primary school traditions, acknowledge the influence of various models of childhood and the effects of new policies in order to develop meeting points which can inform ways forward. Particular views of children and of children as learners and the ways in which educators are charged to carry out their work are essentially political issues.

Perhaps crucially at this time we could ask what model of young children and their learning is implied by a national, universal 3–5 Curriculum Framework or indeed by early literacy interventions as exist in Scotland? What is the political ambition? How is the pre-school child as opposed to the school child, construed?

Policy models in Scotland

In Scotland today the potential for a meeting of the pre-school and primary traditions and curricula has never been more alive, however separate curricula promote different views of learning. In the section 'Children as Learners in the Scottish Curriculum Framework 3–5' it is noted that:

> Children develop understanding in many different ways but they learn best in an environment where they feel safe, secure, confident and have opportunities for enjoyment. Children deepen awareness of themselves as learners by planning, questioning and reflecting. They consolidate this learning when they have time and space to engage in activities in depth. They develop theories through investigation, first hand experience, talk and play.
>
> (The Scottish Office, 1999: 3)

By contrast the 5–14 Curriculum asserts that:

> The task of education is to satisfy the needs of the individual and society and to promote the development of knowledge and understanding, practical skills, attitudes and values.
>
> (Scottish Office Education and Industry Department, 1993: 3)

> In this curriculum the emphasis is on the development of learning skills and techniques, the most important of which are listed as 'the ability to communicate effectively; the ability to locate, access, evaluate and use information; and the capacity to think logically and creatively'.
>
> (SOEID, 1993: 4)

Thus in Scotland the pre-school curriculum focuses on the process of the child constructing knowledge, whilst the primary school curriculum is more focussed on competences and skills of teaching. Freire (1993) describes these positions as a problem seeking approach and a banking approach to education, respectively.

On the one hand then we have the emphasis on the processes of development and learning, and on the other hand we have a focus on skills, knowledge, attitudes and techniques. However, both documents share the aim for children to develop to their fullest potential.

Cultural models

The world in which children grow up is 'socially prestructured': it existed before the child entered it and will continue to exist beyond any individual's childhood (Hundeide, 1993). The passage of children through different phases of childhood will be influenced by the culture in which they live (Bruner and Haste 1987; Vygotsky, 1978; Trevarthen, 1997) and by that culture's ideologies of childhood. In terms of education, views of children and their appropriate education are implicit in the ideologies held and these are reflected in legislation, documentation, educational recommendation and in the approaches taken in schools and classrooms. The ways in which the system, parents, educators and the children themselves think about children and their learning all influence the experience of those children as they travel through our schools. The extent to which each has influence is less clear: whose perspectives should inform early childhood education?

In Scotland the pre-school child can be someone aged from 3.5 years to 4.7 years at the start of the pre-school year through to someone who on entry to school will be between 4.5 and 5.7 years. What assumptions exist about the school entrant, who will after all be anything up to a year older or younger than their neighbour? In this study the majority of children were seen by parents to be competent and ready for school; by educators to be at different points on a long continuum of competence (despite which, in the early months of primary education there was a strong push for sameness in terms of the nature of the experiences offered, the level of content to be taught and social conformity); and by the system to be in need of 'early intervention' which is suggestive of a deficit model of the child, although in fact it is 'early intervention into literacy and numeracy' rather than into the child! At entry to school children had varying degrees of awareness of themselves as learners: perceptions which derived from how they were viewed at home, the responses they met in pre-school and the friendships they had formed.

It is important that we consider the impact of our variously held ideologies on children themselves. By understanding each others' views we may be able to consider the nature of the differences between different stages of education, and to enable the two cultures to meet, to weigh up the possible benefits or hazards in trying to work more closely together and to integrate children's experiences positively (Dahlberg and Talguchi, 1994).

Psychological models

Psychological theory also contributes to an understanding of different curriculum perspectives. The pioneers of the early education tradition held particular views of young children which resulted in a strong growth model. The work of educational philosophers such as Dewey, Peters and Neill further support such a view. This was in contrast to a more historical view of children as empty vessels or *tabulae rasae*. Piaget's work, whilst not determining a particular pedagogy, was in the hands of its interpreters also instrumental in the justification of a child-centred approach to early education which saw children as constructors of their own learning as they passed through certain age linked stages of development. Donaldson's work (1978) had an early influence in Scotland and supported a growing view that learning should make 'human sense' for children: that it should be embedded, with educators working towards an increasing capacity to dissemble.

Trevarthen's work on inter-subjectivity (Trevarthen and Aitken, 2001) offers a foundation for considering the importance of early emotional interaction and interchange between care-giver and child which has led to him now considering the importance of 'teacherese': interactions between teachers and children as indicative of the quality of learning environments for our children. Child–parent dialogue (Wells, 1986) is significant in children's early learning. The focus on curriculum content which dominates current early primary practice is mediated by more attention to the nature of the interactions: in terms of reciprocity, power sharing and exchange of ideas . This allows children to construct their knowledge with support of the culture and the more experienced other as proposed by Vygotsky (1978) and Bruner and Haste (1987).

In any psychological model of learning which espouses children as constructors of their learning, pupil–teacher dialogue will be one of the determinants of children's experience. By studying the amount of talk in classrooms as well as the nature of that talk and the child–teacher balance we may be able to gain insights into the contribution of social and cultural classroom norms on children's learning.

Astington (1994) writes that around the age of five, through a process of discovery of their own and others' mental states, children have normally reached concepts of 'a mind-independent reality'. She claims they recognise that different people may have different constructs of the same happenings or reality and that beliefs are subject to change. She also makes a strong connection between language development and capacity to understand mental states. This last seems to be an important idea when some very young children are starting out in formalised, if not already formal, education. It is in a more formalised system that children may be faced with disembedded ideas. Children who are alert to mental state under-standing, may be more able to read the social situation of the school, or the stories others tell of school and to better speculate on how it will be in school, thus being more prepared and resilient to change should it occur, and more able to relate to others' intentions for cognitive tasks (Dunlop, 2001).

Can these perspectives of policy, culture, and psychology, come together to support a conceptual framework of early years which will provide young children with continuity, progression in their learning, coherence and relevance in their curriculum?

Research on the children's experience in pre-school and in primary

The experience of four children in transition from pre-school (nursery) settings into their primary education are described. This helps identify what happens for children when parent, pre-school educator, primary school educators, local authority policy views and children's views of learners are taken into account. The evidence is drawn from parent interviews and questionnaires, staff semi-structured interviews in pre-school and early primary education, classroom observations, video episodes focusing on language and communication as windows on children's learning, researcher assessments and child group interviews (Dunlop, 2002; Dunlop and Fraser, 2001). Each of these elements has something to offer in terms of varying perspectives on young children's learning. Analysis of classroom discourse (Potter and Wetherall, 1987; Hicks, 1996) and reflection on power relationships in classrooms (Manke, 1997) reveal how it is for children in their early education settings.

The twenty-eight children in the main study between them experienced sixteen different pre-school/primary pairings of settings at transition to school. Of the four children mentioned, three attended the same pre-school setting and the fourth came from a different setting. Katie, Ruby and Colin's pre-school and primary experience demonstrated the highest continuity of experience on all dimensions: setting, relationships and curriculum out of all possible pairings: the two teachers worked well and closely together. For Trevor, the paired experience of pre-school and primary was highly discontinuous. In each case the child's personal experience of continuity or discontinuity was influenced by personal qualities as well as by the nature of these two early experiences. Katie's experience, feelings and response were highly continuous, as were Colin's. Ruby and Trevor experienced greater discontinuity. Whilst Trevor found the new setting quite a challenge, it was a favourable new experience. Ruby was more retiring and took much longer to settle in confidently. In each case Mrs Devine had acquired useful knowledge about each child and their previous experience and tuned her approach accordingly.

Children's views of themselves as learners

At nursery

Trevor (4.4) spends half this research visit rushing around the room, being noisy and sticking his tongue out at the camera. For the other half he sits by himself in a corner unwilling to participate. He has been fluctuating from one extreme to the other for some weeks. 'We do too much sitting' he says of nursery, and 'you can only talk about what the teacher chooses'.

Katie(4.8) spends the last part of the morning writing letters and invitations. 'Amy's going to be five. She's asked me to her party. We're making more invitations so that everyone can come. You have to put all the names on. I can write names. Some of them I have to copy and some I know in my head.'

Ruby (4.4) dresses up. She parades in front of the mirror in leotard and purple tights (having taken some time to extract both her legs from the single leg of the leotard that she had put them through). 'You'd better hurry up dear' she says to her friend. 'Get your shoes on, we're going out to the hall for aerobics. We won't need to change when we get there. I'll bring a shopping list and we can stop at the bakers for our biscuits and drinks. We'll need 3p each: bring 5p.'

Colin (5.3) plays with the construction. He collaborates with a group of others, deciding where to place each piece. If there is any conflict of interest as they build, he supports the others by saying ' I'll decide for you: that's easy for me'.

At home

Trevor (4.5) has been matching like with like during the assessment process undertaken at his home by the researcher. Nearly at the end of the game, he contemplates the four remaining pictures: two leaves and two fish. He has easily matched the previous eighteen pairs of cards, but now he looks puzzled. The researcher wonders if she has missed something or if her concentration had lapsed. She prompts Trevor:

R: You're nearly finished Trevor: can you match the last pairs?
T: No it's a bit of a problem.
R: Tell me about it.
T: Well, do you see these two? I can't decide what they are (he points to the leaves).
R: Tell me what you think they are.
T: Well that's the trouble, I can't tell if they're sycamores or oak leaves. They're kind of small, I guess they must be oak leaves (he puts them aside and now looks closely at the fish).
T: I think I'll look these up: you can't tell from these pictures what they are. I mean, they might be basking sharks or they might be great whites (he goes to find his encyclopedia of sharks).
T: Do you know how many varieties there are? I think there are 192 in this book. I like sharks. I think I like the hammerheads the best, but these are more like basking sharks: look!

Katie (4.9) is looking at the book *The Hungry Caterpillar*, she turns and says 'We always start at the left'. A short while later she offers to show how she can write her name 'Oh dear, I'm always doing that', she says as she writes the K back to front and at the right side of the page. 'I have to tell myself to remember which hand I like to have my pencil in: it's the left you know, and then I start at the left of the page and it's the right way round.'

Ruby (4.6) 'I love story books, I read and read and read them, I even read them to Liam, but he's a baby and he doesn't really understand. He bends the books back and I tell him 'you have to hold it properly Liam. He can't read yet. I can, but just stories I know.'

Colin (5.4) considers himself one of the big boys, 'I've got friends in the primary too, I like construction and stories, I can't read yet, but I'll learn at school'.

At primary school

In the early days of primary school the class teacher and children were observed at various points of the school day and engaged in a range of learning and teaching situations.

Teacher led activity

The children have been enjoying a whole class session during which they have been sequencing numbers and later words. The teacher has made this into a lot of fun, with children actively participating in one or other activity by taking responsibility for a large sized number or word card. They love the nonsense of numbers in the wrong sequence and of moving each other around to get the 1–10 sequence correct. As many sequences as possible are tried with their early 5 word core vocabulary of look, see, can, it, I. Pleasurable laughter resounds round the room: once again children are actively involved. Trevor (4.8) is a bit loud and doesn't get chosen, but contributes at every turn. Katie (4.11) volunteers several times and then has the chance to join in. Ruby (4.7) sits very quiet, smiling, but looking as if she'd prefer not to be chosen: her teacher is aware of this, smiles reassuringly, but at this stage doesn't force a response. Colin (5.7) is pleased to be involved and does what's asked of him.

Child led activity

Trevor (4.8) and his partner Sally are working on a paired reading task as a follow up to a whole class reading session which emphasised through active participation of the children, the opportunities to create meaningful sentences from a limited sight vocabulary. They had a bag containing a range of single word cards, and eight sentence cards with which to match them. The teacher had pointed out that there were not enough words in the little bag to complete all the sentences – the children would have to negotiate with each other on how to tackle the task and how to complete all the sentences by borrowing from those they had been able to complete first. Tom insisted Sally had got it wrong, and refused to render any of the completed sentences incomplete by lending or borrowing a needed card. He interpreted the problem in human terms, and claimed 'We haven't got 'here', someone must have nicked it!' and to the teacher 'Mrs Devine, we haven't got here, I mean (louder) WE HAVEN'T GOT ENOUGH OF 'HERE'!'

Katie (4.11) had completed her colouring in of the new letter learned that morning: C in a cat form. Ready to cut it out she started with her left hand. Her concentration was intense while she stood to do this task. It was laborious. After some time she changed the scissors to her right hand, smiled, and completed the task. She sought out the teacher to show her the completed work.

Ruby (4.7) was struggling with the colouring in. Katie came back beside her and encouraged her to persist.

Colin (5.7) found himself in a group who were asked to create a house out of a huge Lego collection. There was much discussion in the group before they started: on each occasion when there was a difference of opinion, Colin mediated. The group was proud of its creation and ready to explain their thinking and resolution of problems to the teacher who discussed the height, need for windows, insulation and possible price of the house with them. Later she developed an imaginative context of an estate agent's office in the classroom.

Perspectives on children as learners

The parents views of their children as learners

The parents of these four children were confident that their children were ready for school. They highlighted a range of home learning opportunities, their views of their children as individuals and learners and some concerns about the transition into school. Whilst often seeing their children as eager for learning and socially competent, they expressed concerns about social conformity, their capacity to sit still, the suitability of classroom organisation, and in one case 'the absolute power of the teacher'. They found their children had endless curiosity, good personalities and a sense of fun. Their views largely corresponded with how the pre-school practitioners also viewed these children.

Structured interviews with parents shed light on how parents see their children as learners. In keeping with Howe *et al.* (1999) findings, emphasis was placed on children's social integration and readiness for school. Parents were asked about children's learning and attitudes: including the child's use of time, levels of involvement, child-parent interaction, taking of responsibility for self-help routines, the child's behaviour towards a range of people in the family and community including strangers, and learning at home. Parents indicated the extent to which children showed competence in these areas: their responses were given on a four point scale (1 – low; 4 – high) (Table 8.1).

Children who were highly socially oriented proved to be more comfortable with all aspects of transition. Children whose home profiles indicated high levels of involvement with adults combined with high levels of talk did not necessarily find themselves or their verbal competence appreciated in school: this depended on the degree of social conformity they could demonstrate in the group setting.

Table 8.1 Key features of learning at home

Key feature	Trevor	Katie	Ruby	Colin
Uses time productively	4	4	3	2
Concentration and involvement	3	3	4	3
Level of talk with parents	4	4	4	4
Self-help routines	4	4	3	4
Child's behaviour towards others	2	4	3	3
Learning at home	4	4	3	3

Educators' views of children as learners

Pre-school and school educators' were interviewed about approaches to continuity in transition. Questionnaires on the teaching of literacy also allowed for comparisons between pre-school and primary practitioners' views of children's learning. Classroom observations augmented the picture of children as learners by tapping into their actual experience as well as the 'planned for' experience and contributed to a full picture of actual pre-school and primary provision.

The following elements were explored in the semi-structured interviews with pre-school practitioners and primary teachers:

- Aims and philosophy
- Responsibilities
- Present practice
- Descriptions of approach
- Teaching style
- Groupings
- Effects of curriculum guidelines
- Methodology implied
- Structured play/variety of activities/choice
- Teacher assessment and record keeping
- Planning
- Pastoral continuity
- Curricular continuity
- People important in transition
- People important in continuity
- Knowledge of other sector's curriculum
- Knowledge of other sector's practice
- Support for transition
- Preparation for staff offering support
- Other possibilities
- Intentions for leavers/ in start up days
- Skills of children leaving/starting
- What routines do they need to learn
- Taking account of learning/differentiation
- Information passed on
- Other information liked
- Cross visits
- The significance of pre-school learning and experience
- Liaison
- Contact with parents
- Knowledge of individuals
- Variation of approach to cater for individuals

A comparison of educators', parents' and children's views

Whilst a common language was used by educators in both pre-school and primary, it was clear at the start of the study that the concepts expressed held different meanings according to the sector in which the staff member taught and their personal philosophy. Differing views of children as learners will influence the educational experiences they have. The extent to which such views do have influence is less clear: whose perspectives should inform early childhood education?

How close are the views of children as learners held by pre-school and early primary practitioners?

While primary teachers valued the importance of the nursery experience, there was a wide discrepancy between their views of the capabilities of the new entrant and the views nursery staff held of leavers. Information about school entrants did not always reach the classroom teachers at a time when it would have been most useful and classroom observations revealed difficulties in providing for continuity of experience: mainly because of the lack of knowledge of practice in the 'other' sector. This lack of knowledge extended in some cases to little knowledge of the curriculum as documented, delivered and experienced. Consequently it became evident that pre-school and primary practitioners might espouse the same principles and philosophies, but in reality their views of children as learners could differ markedly. A focus on 'adult expectations, attributions and framing of child activity' (Burman, 1994: 26) becomes apparent, leading to sector-specific views of learners.

What opportunities were there for parents to share their views of their children as learners with the pre-school and primary staff?

Parents felt confident that the pre-school practitioners knew their children well. They felt informed about the pre-school curriculum, but at the point of transition felt less knowledgeable about the primary school curriculum. Frequent staff–parent contacts were common in pre-school and this raised both doubts and expectations of similar contact at the primary school stage. The informal contact rarely survived beyond the children graduating to the full primary day and was replaced with formal consultations, although many parents had found the staff in Primary 1 (the first year of compulsory schooling) approachable and regretted there were so few opportunities to meet and talk. Many parents were sympathetic to the scale of the task undertaken by primary teachers and admiring of their success. It was clear however that the possibility of practitioners knowing children as individuals and being in a position to develop shared views of those individual children with their parents was far more likely at the pre-school stage.

What opportunities were there for children to express their views of themselves as learners, and to what extent did adult assumptions or expectations colour these opportunities ?

The new Curriculum 3–5 has reinforced and further developed understandings about working with a system of planning that is responsive to children's interests and concerns. Intensive staff development at the pre-school stage in the particular local authority had brought major shifts in expectation from pre-school staff. Five key aspects of children's development and learning are identified in the curriculum. The first aspect that was approached in this way was the communication and language aspect of the curriculum. As the main study children proceeded through their first year of primary the advent of 'Early Intervention' brought benefits in key early primary teachers understanding of pre-school practice and views of the primary entrant began to change. This was enhanced by the local authority's response to a number of recommendations from the researcher including support by nursery staff in the early weeks of primary education (Dunlop and Fraser, 2001).

What account is taken of children's voices?

As knowledge, communication, information sharing and relationships between sectors began to change, children's learning and their ways of learning were more fully discussed. Over time this meant that some teachers were more able to support children to make a fuller contribution in the primary class. This was particularly evident in the class which the four children cited in this paper entered. Analysis of classroom discourse has shown the extent to which children's views of themselves as capable learners are fostered in pre-school and primary settings. There is some indication that increased participation in planning and organisation, attention to contexts for learning, more attention to children's learning styles, the value placed on co-construction of knowledge as a teacher–child collaboration, the maintenance of levels of independence achieved in pre-school, time for talk and storying, and opportunities for active learning are all instrumental in a process which pays more respect to children themselves, and to children as learners.

Reflections on differing views of children at school entry: teachers, parents, children

Differing views of children as learners are bound to occur as children form a variety of learning relationships, but disparity of views amongst educators are unlikely to be in children's best interests. We need to find ways to share policies, to understand each other's ideologies and respect but integrate them, to experience each sector that children themselves experience and to know and value the powerful learning that children bring with them to pre-school and school.

These meeting points are important. The origins of our views of children as learners are also important. We must know the extent to we have been making assumptions about children's learning; the extent to which we which we are influenced by theory and critically revisit it and the extent to which research into current practice can inform the way ahead.

The value of the continuity that communicating early educators can achieve across sectors and with the home will make a vital contribution to children's developing views of themselves as thinkers, learners and language users. Evidence from this study shows that children will be more able to make sense of the curriculum, the relationships and the settings in which and through which they are expected to learn if the people responsible for their learning can develop shared views and provide accordingly. One of the striking features of the Continuity Study (Dunlop, 1996–2000) is the way in which it reveals the competence of the school entrant. A shared conceptual framework of the child who is about to enter school is badly needed in early education (Broadhead, 1995) – shared between parents and teachers at different stages, but also between educators at pre-school and primary stages and taking account of both. Without such shared understanding children will find a dissonance in how they are viewed from competent and accomplished people with a variety of strengths and needs to incompetent novices unable to exercise responsibility or make contributions in the interests of their own learning.

Pre-school educators', primary educators' and home educators' views of children as learners differ: let's find the meeting places – conceptually and practically – but avoid the push for sameness.

References

Astington, J.W. (1993) *The Child's Discovery of Mind*. London: Fontana Press.

Astington, J.W. (2000) *Minds in the Making. Essays in Honor of David R. Olsen*. Oxford: Blackwell.

Broadhead, P. (ed.) (1995) *Researching the Early Years Continuum*. BERA Dialogues 12. Clevedon: Multi-lingual matters.

Bruner, J. and Haste, H. (eds) (1987) *Making Sense. The Child's Construction of the World*. London: Routledge.

Burman, E. (1994) *Deconstructing Developmental Psychology*. London: Routledge.

Dahlberg, G. and Talguchi, H.L. (1994) *Pre-school and School. Two Different Traditions and the Vision of a Meeting Place*. Special print from Appendix 3 to the report *Grunden för livslångt lärande. En barnmogen skola* (*The Foundations for Lifelong Learning. A Child Ready School*) Statens Offentliga Utredningar.

Donaldson, M. (1978) *Children's Minds*. Glasgow: Fontana Collins.

Dunlop, A.W.A. (2001) 'Children's thinking about transitions to school'. Paper presented at the 11th Annual Conference of the European Educational Research Association. Alkmaar.

Dunlop, A.W.A. (2002) 'A study into continuity and progression for young children in early educational transitions'. Unpublished PhD thesis, University of Strathclyde, Glasgow.

Dunlop, A.W.A. and Fraser, I. (2001) 'Collaboration in promoting continuity and progression for young children: the impact of research on practice in one local authority'. Unpublished paper, University of Strathclyde, Glasgow.

Freire, P. (1993) *Pedagogy of the Oppressed*. London: Penguin.

Hicks, D. (1996) *Discourse, Learning and Schooling*. Cambridge: Cambridge University Press.

Howe, C., Foot, H., Cheyne, B., Terras, M. and Rattray, C. (1999) 'What do parents Really want from pre-school education?'. In *Pre-school Educational Research. Linking Policy with Practice*. Edinburgh: Scottish Executive Education Department.

Hundeide, K. (1993) 'Intersubjectivity and interpretive background in children's development and interaction', *European Journal of Psychology of Education* VIII(4), 439–50.

Manke, M.P. (1997) *Classroom Power Relations: Understanding Student–Teacher Interaction*. London: Lawrence Erlbaum Associates.

Potter, J. and Wetherall, M. (1987) *Discourse and Social Psychology. Beyond Attitudes and Behaviour*. London: Sage.

Scottish Consultative Council on the Curriculum. (1999) *The Curriculum Framework for Children 3–5*. Dundee: SCCC.

Scottish Office Education and Industry Department (SOCID) (1993) *The National Guidelines for Curriculum and Assessment in Scotland for Education 5–14*. Edinburgh: HSMO.

Trevarthen, C. (1997) 'The curricular conundrum: prescription versus the Comenius principle'. In Dunlop, A.W.A. and Hughes, A. (eds), *Pre-School Curriculum, Policy, Practice and Proposals*. Glasgow: University of Strathclyde.

Trevarthen, C. and Aitken, K.J. (2001) 'Infant intersubjectivity: research, theory and clinical applications'. *Annual Research Review, Journal of Clinical Psychology and Psychiatry* 42(1), 3–48.

Vygotsky, L.S. (1978) *Mind in Society*. Cambridge, MA and London: Harvard.

Wells, G. (1986) *The Meaning Makers. London: Children Learning Language and Using Language to Learn*. London: Hodder and Stoughton Educational.

Chapter 9

Planning transition programmes

Kay Margetts

Children entering school face a setting that is qualitatively different from their previous experiences in terms of the curriculum, the setting and the people. There is concern that these differences may impact on children's adjustment to school and disrupt their learning and development processes. When children adjust adequately in the first year of schooling much of the initial stress associated with transition can be overcome, and children are more likely to be successful in their future progress than a child who has difficulty adjusting to the new situation. The impacts and stresses associated with transition to schooling are being recognised by many teachers and administrators, and transition programmes are being implemented to minimise the adjustments required for success in the first year of schooling.

It is important that transition programmes are carefully planned. How well children adjust to school depends on the first links between the child, the family and the school. The kinds of experiences children encounter as they make sense of relatively new surroundings, routines and procedures, and learn what behaviour is considered appropriate, may have far reaching effects on their development and their adjustment to school. The more familiar and sensitive the new setting, the easier the transition. Transition programmes should therefore create an appropriate degree of continuity between early childhood and school experiences and develop strategies to help children adjust to school.

In 1992, the Directorate of School Education's review of school-entry age in the state of Victoria, Australia recognised that the transition to the first year of schooling is one of five significant factors influencing a child's ability to achieve initial success at school. The Directorate recommended that schools develop transition programmes for all children beginning school and that these programmes should create links between children, families, pre-school services and the school (MRSEAV, 1992). The response has been varied, but the anecdotal evidence from schools that have developed carefully planned transition programmes, sensitive to the needs of children and their families and the community in which they are situated, has been very positive in terms of children's adjustment to school and the development of links between families, schools and pre-school services.

Transition programmes

Transition programmes are variously identified as strategies and procedures for ensuring the smooth placement and adjustment of children to school. They involve activities initiated by schools or pre-schools to bridge the gap and create links between home, pre-school and school. While transition programmes will vary from community to community and school to school, the effectiveness and quality of these programmes depends largely on communication and collaboration between all people involved in the process.

An investigation of processes in the planning of effective transition programmes characterised by low levels of child distress and high levels of teacher and parent satisfaction revealed the following key elements:

* collaboration with other people/services;
* clear goals and objectives;
* understanding of the challenges facing children and the adjustments they need to make as they move into the first year of schooling;
* written plans and strategies;
* evaluation.

Collaboration with others

The first step in planning effective transition programmes is to establish a transition team. The team can be made up of teachers, parents, and specialists from the school and a range of pre-school services including kindergartens, childcare centres and early childhood specialist support services. School representatives usually comprise the early years co-ordinator, early years staff and parent representatives. Members from pre-school services generally include teachers, co-ordinators and other interested staff and parents. The importance of the interconnectedness of home, pre-school and school experiences needs to be acknowledged, coupled with increased professional respect between the pre-school and school sectors. An openness to multiple perspectives adds to the richness of the planning process and resulting programmes.

The team should meet initially to acknowledge the importance of transition programmes and the desire to work collaboratively in a way that values and builds on the involvement and strengths of all members. The following meetings should establish clear goals, identify problems and concerns, and develop transition strategies.

Establishing a transition team can be difficult and may depend on one or two key players to get the process started. These key people may be from either pre-schools or school. It is important that the team has the support of the administrators and other teachers of the services represented. The effectiveness of the team may depend on the facilities and resources made available for staff and others to participate, and the interest and encouragement of non-team members in the transition processes.

One teacher recalled,

> I was the early years co-ordinator at the local primary school and realised that transition was important. I approached the school principal and the school council who gave enthusiastic support and approval for me to form a transition team. I visited the local pre-schools and childcare centres and spoke to the teachers about my ideas. I also wrote to all families of children enrolled for the following year asking for parents to volunteer to be team members. A team was formed consisting of the assistant principal, two early years teachers, a school council member, three parents of pre-schoolers, two pre-school teachers, a coordinator of a childcare centre, an occupational therapist and myself. At our first meeting we spent time getting to know each other and expressing ideas and concerns about transition.

In some regions of Victoria, transition networks have been established where representatives from a number of schools, pre-schools, local council, support services and parents meet at least once a term to discuss transition issues and plan programmes in relation to the broader community context. These transition networks focus on sharing and maximising resources and enhancing communication and collaboration between services and key people. Given that children from one pre-school may be enrolled at many different schools, opportunities to network and carefully coordinate transition schedules are important. In many cases transition networks provide professional development for staff on a wide range of related issues and help to overcome some of the divisions that exist between pre-school and school sectors.

Establishing clear goals and objectives

It is important to develop clear goals and objectives for transition programmes. This is an opportunity to develop a vision of a successful transition programme not only for the children but also for staff, parents, pre-school services, and other groups represented on the transition team. This process can be achieved through consultation with others and provides an opportunity to develop cohesiveness and a strong sense of doing something of value.

The following are sample goals that can guide the planning of transition strategies:

- to promote the speedy adjustment of the child and the family to the new situation;
- to encourage the child's independence and successful functioning in the new environment;
- to support and inform the family in the process;
- to promote collaboration between family, school, pre-school and community;
- to encourage the active involvement of children, parents, family, school, pre-school and community in the transition process.

Understanding the challenges facing children and the adjustments they need to make as they move from home or pre-school into school

Before developing transition strategies, the next step is to identify the challenges facing children and the adjustments they need to make as they commence the first year of schooling. It has been widely acknowledged that problems can occur as a result of differences or discontinuities between previous experiences and the new school. Starting school involves coping with change, with the uncertainties and tensions that accompany it, and responding appropriately to those demands. Children must adjust to strange buildings and classrooms, new school and teacher expectations, new academic challenges, and they need to mix with a new and more diverse group of children. When the impacts and stresses of these challenges are identified, transition programmes can be planned to minimise the adjustments required for successful transition into the first year of schooling.

Class sizes and the ratio of staff to children changes at school. There is now only one adult per class. There is more verbal instruction, a focus on literacy and numeracy, and the need to use pencils and other small equipment. There is an increase in waiting times, and the daily schedule is more structured, with more formal rules and routines.

As children move to specialist classrooms each with a different teacher they need to adjust to the different attitudes and expectations of each teacher. They are faced with large groups of children of different ages and size especially during assembly and playtime, and they are confronted with the challenges of making new friends.

Toilets are often located away from classrooms and play areas. There are more buildings and the playgrounds are bigger. There is often only limited adult supervision in the playgrounds. Physical activities are generally restricted to physical education lessons and playtime involving a lot of running, climbing and ball games.

Parents may be confused about their own role and the new routines and procedures associated with the school. Parents' expectations of children often change as children commence schooling with pressure on children to read, write and demonstrate numeracy skills. Parental uncertainty and pressure can add to the child's stress.

Children from rural areas often have to travel by school bus, and spend long hours away from home. Children with working parents may also be away from home for long periods of time and may need to make multiple adjustments as they commence before and after school care as well as the first year of schooling.

Developing a written plan and strategies

An effective transition programme should provide the implementation of the best transition practices and therefore result in successful adjustment to school. It should involve systematic, individualised, timely and collaborative planning. A written plan should include a description of the transition programme along with time lines or dates and specific responsibilities of key personnel. The written plan provides a valuable source of information for the community and supports the smooth running of the programme and helps to avoid confusion. Furthermore, the written plan provides a basis for evaluation of the programme.

The timing of transition programmes will vary from school to school and even child to child. The schedule of school visits should be flexible and responsive to the needs of children and parents and pre-school services. Working parents often experience difficulty attending meetings during the daytime and children in child-care may not be able to attend school visits. Some schools provide evening and weekend transition activities in response to these issues. While many transition programmes are implemented in the last two months of the school year prior to commencement, a significant number of schools conduct parent information sessions and school visits over a period of six months.

In supporting children's adjustment to school and addressing the challenges that may disrupt children's learning and development, transition programmes should include strategies that attempt to retain the benefits of pre-school programmes, reduce the stress children might experience commencing school, create an appropriate degree of continuity as children move into school, respond to the variety of children's backgrounds and experiences, and provide positive experiences. These strategies should respond to and reflect child, family and community characteristics and needs.

When developing a written plan and strategies each of the following key elements should be included: preparation of children for school; involvement of parents in the transition; communication/collaboration between pre-school and school staff; and programme continuity.

Preparation of children

Transition programmes should prepare pre-schoolers for the demands and challenges of school and strategies can be implemented before and during the commencement of schooling. One of the most important influences on learning is the setting in which it occurs. If the setting is familiar, children are more likely to adjust to new demands and expectations. When children are prepared for making the transition to school they gain self-confidence and are more likely to succeed.

Transition programmes should include many formal and informal opportunities for children and their families to visit the school before commencement. Research conducted in Victoria (Margetts, 1997) revealed a significant association between children's adjustment to school and multiple opportunities for children and families to visit and become familiar with the school prior to commencement. Where schools conducted high numbers of transition activities, children experienced fewer problem behaviours than children who attended schools with a limited number of transition opportunities. This research suggests that children and families should be provided with multiple opportunities to familiarise themselves with the school environment and expectations, and to facilitate the gradual preparation of pre-schoolers for the challenges and demands of school.

First-hand experiences of the new situation prior to commencement, allow children time to assimilate and accommodate the old with the new, and to talk about their feelings with sensitive adults, in preparing them for the challenges they face. A series of visits provides children with opportunities to know what teachers expect of them, to become familiar with the new environment including toilets, buildings and play areas, to identify differences between pre-school and school and the adaptations required, to participate in classroom activities, to practise skills necessary for school, and to meet new friends and develop support systems.

School experiences can be varied. As well as visits and school tours for children with their parents, pre-schools can arrange visits to local schools to listen to the orchestra or band, to use the library, art room or other facilities, and to participate in classrooms and play-times. Buddy systems can be implemented with children currently in the first year of schooling taking responsibility for the children in transition. This is particularly effective given the similarities of age and play interests. Other strategies include opportunities for pre-school children to have lunch at the school, and to attend school dress-up days or festivals. When children visit schools with their pre-school group they are provided with school experiences in the company and security of familiar playmates and staff. These visits should not exclude children who will not be attending the particular school but may be seen in the context of an excursion – a valuable learning experience.

One school commenced their transition programme in the second quarter of the school year with Grade 5 children visiting the local pre-schools to play with children, and pre-schoolers attending the Easter Bonnet Parade and other celebrations. In the final quarter of the year pre-schoolers attended the school for one hour on a fortnightly basis in groups of twenty to participate in classroom activities. Fortnightly visits to the school library also occurred when children could listen to stories, watch a video or make their own books. Because the school had a canteen, one transition visit provided children with practice of lining up and conducting their own purchase.

As children commence school they are required to function independently, develop relationships with staff and peers, and to behave in ways that are appropriate for their class and school and involve conforming to rules. In helping children make the transition to school it is important to identify the social skills and behaviours that contribute to children's adjustment. Strategies can be implemented at pre-school and at home to promote these skills.

A recent study (Margetts, 2000) identified a range of social skills and behaviours associated with children's adjustment to the first year of schooling. Findings suggested that when children exhibited a range of social skills associated with co-operation, initiating interactions, and self-control they were more likely to adjust easily to school. Skills associated with cooperation included ignoring peer distractions, attending to and following instructions, putting away materials, and the ability to wait. Assertive- or initiating-type social skills included inviting others to join in activities, complimenting peers, initiating conversations and introducing oneself to others also contribute to early school adjustment. Skills associated with self-control included the ability to control one's temper in conflict situations, and to respond appropriately to peer pressure. When children exhibited frequent aggressive, anxious and restless behaviours they were more likely to experience difficulties adjusting to school than children who did not or rarely demonstrated these behaviours. Aggressive behaviours included getting angry easily, talking back to adults, arguing and fighting with others. Anxious behaviours included those associated with sadness or perceived low self-esteem. Restless behaviours included disturbing activities, not listening to others, fidgeting and moving excessively, and being easily distracted.

In supporting the development of social skills it is important that children at pre-school and home are encouraged and assisted to interact with peers and adults in positive ways. This should include support in conflict and non-conflict situations. Children should be encouraged to share, take turns and co-operate, to ask for help from adults, to listen to others, and follow reasonable instructions.

Children should be supported in developing self-confidence, and have opportunities to experience success when trying new things and coping with the unexpected. When children are given consistent guidance and support in being responsible for controlling their feelings and behaving in acceptable ways without disturbing or hurting others, they are more likely to exhibit self-control. Children's independence is further supported when they take responsibility for their actions and their belongings. They should be encouraged to persevere with difficult tasks such as completing a puzzle, working out how to prevent a block tower from collapsing, or practising hitting a target with a ball.

Other strategies can include pre-school staff and parents delaying and decreasing their attention and praise, reducing instructions and prompts, increasing independence, assigning roles and responsibilities, and including school uniforms and bags in dramatic play areas. It is important that pre-school staff are familiar with school practices so that they can accurately respond to children's questions and establish realistic expectations.

Having friends in the same class can help children adjust to the demands of school. In the Victorian study (Margetts, 1997), children who commenced school with a familiar playmate in the same class demonstrated more social skills, fewer problem behaviours, and were rated more academically competent than children who did not have a familiar playmate in the same class. Having a familiar playmate in the same class also compensated for deleterious factors, such as being young in age, being a boy, attendance at childcare, and not speaking English at home, which placed a child at risk of not adjusting well to the first year of school. The significance of having a familiar playmate in the same class should not be ignored and strategies implemented to ensure that children commence school with a familiar playmate wherever possible.

A smooth transition may also be promoted through children continuing their existing friendships inside and outside the new school environment, or participating in a buddy system (Ladd and Price, 1987). Strategies should be developed for promoting the continuation of existing friendships or the development of new friendships. These friendships can be facilitated when school staff introduce new parents to each other, provide special 'get-to-know-you' playtimes, and encourage parents to arrange play opportunities to foster emerging friendships. To minimise the social adjustments children need to make as they commence school, some schools are now allocating children to classes based on their pre-school classes and thus keeping children who are familiar with each other, together.

Parent involvement

The relationship between parents and teachers is important across all levels of the school but even more so at the commencement of schooling. The continuity of parent involvement in their child's education benefits the children and a joint effort between school and home helps effect a smooth transition.

It is important that parents are informed about school procedures and expectations, and teachers listen to parents' concerns and goals for their children. Informed parents are less likely to be stressed about their child's transition to school and more able to support their child in overcoming their confusion and frustration and in adapting to the new environment.

Parent involvement in the transition process can include orientation visits for parents and children, providing parents with verbal and written information about the school, opportunities for parents to become familiar with the staff and parent organisations within the school, informing parents about their rights and responsibilities, time to talk to teachers, helping parents understand the transition process from the child's perspective, identifying skills and behaviours related to successful school adjustment, suggesting activities that may assist in preparing children for school, talks at local pre-schools and childcare centres with both pre-school and school staff as speakers, and social events before and after the commencement of school. It is important that parents are given information about the procedures of the first day at school and what is expected of them and their child. One transition team produced and distributed a newsletter to keep parents updated about relevant transition information.

While the ultimate responsibility for planning these events lies with the transition team, school parent associations can contribute to the planning and organisation of parent and family focused transition strategies.

Communication between staff

In developing smooth transitions, staff from both sectors benefit when they have information about and understand something of each child's background and prior experiences. This information is best transmitted when there is ongoing communication between staff at the variety of pre-school services and schools. In this way partnerships between schools and pre-school personnel can be established and facilitate a strengthening of knowledge and expertise between teachers.

The sharing of information and collaborative planning for children's transition to school can occur formally and informally. Formal methods included the transfer of records with information including children's levels of social, physical and intellectual development and an estimate of their needs; staff visiting each other's programmes to discuss children; collaborative planning of transition programmes; and membership of early childhood or transition networks. Some schools invite pre-school and childcare staff to visit children in their classes within the first month of commencing school. This provides opportunities for staff to share valuable information particularly in regard to behavioural or learning concerns.

Programme continuity

Transition adjustment and consequential problems for children starting school can be reduced if continuity of intent and learning is promoted through the provision of developmentally appropriate and familiar programmes. As part of the planning process these strategies can be devised and implemented in the early weeks of children commencing schooling. A link with prior learning experiences can be supported by the provision of messy play, art and dramatic play areas in the classroom. The provision of outdoor play materials involving water play or sand play, and same-age play spaces supervised by adults may also assist children's adjustment to school. Associated with this approach is the recognition and provision of time for children to practise and consolidate new skills and behaviours.

Following the commencement of school a flexible schedule of attendance and a gradual introduction to school has been advocated to enable children to participate more successfully in school activities. In Victoria, children commencing the first year of schooling attend for half a day for the first week, from 9.00am until 2.00pm for the first two months and fulltime thereafter.

Evaluation

To assist in the development of sensitive, responsive and effective transition programmes, and to determine the success or otherwise of these initiatives, evaluation processes are critical. Evaluation should occur in relation to the aims and objectives developed by the transition team, transition structures, processes and desired outcomes.

Feedback can be obtained through the use of carefully devised questionnaires or interviews and may include information from children, parents, pre-school and school staff and other people involved in the transition process, including the extent to which their various expectations were met. It can be helpful to establish indicators of effective transition in the initial planning stages to provide a focus for evaluation processes. Indicators may also include indexes of children's development and functioning, and child, parent and teacher expectations.

Additionally, the transition team should be encouraged to conduct their own debriefing session where they honestly identify difficulties and successes including management issues, and discuss future directions. Evaluations can occur during the last month of the school year and also near the end of the first term of the new school year. They should be finalised prior to planning for the next transition programme.

The information received through the evaluation process should be seen as a valuable part of planning for effective transition and a basis for constructive change or the strengthening of existing strategies.

What some schools are doing

Hawthorn West Primary School is located in an inner urban area. This school is one of many schools recognising that the stress associated with starting school is reduced when children and their parents are involved in carefully planned transition activities with many opportunities to visit the school and become familiar with the new environment. The school places emphasis on the continuity of parent involvement in their child's education and values the strong sense of community within the school. The children and parents participate in a range of formal and informal activities. The school runs a four-week transition programme in the second last month of the school year and also provides a range of more informal social activities including an end of year barbecue. During the transition programme children and parents visit the school once a week. Children participate in classroom activities, parents are provided with information and are welcomed into the classrooms where they also have opportunities to chat to teachers. During these sessions teachers observe the children and make notes about children's level of functioning and friendships to assist them in allocating children to classes for the following year. There is also a mentor programme where new families are matched with existing families as a basis for building friendships and relationships. The transition co-ordinator commented,

> When children have many opportunities to visit the school there are very few tears and the children are confident and more independent when they start. Parents seem more willing to trust us to look after their children. The transition programme benefits the school as well as the children. Staff are able to get to know the children and identify their strengths and needs. This helps with placing children into classes. The visits give children and parents the opportunity to be more aware and feel comfortable with how the school operates and to meet the staff and other families.

Belgrave South Primary School is situated in a semi-rural outer metropolitan area. This school introduced a comprehensive transition programme in 1998 in which children and parents had at least ten opportunities to become familiar with the school and develop a sense of belonging. The school received such favourable feedback that they ran the programme again in 1999. Visits to the school start in the second half of the school year. In the last quarter of the school year children participate in regular classroom activities and routines each Friday morning. At the same time parents are given information about different aspects of the school's organisation and are able to talk with staff and members of the parent association, as well as staff from the welfare and outside school hours programmes. The principal stresses,

> It is important to work out what parent needs are. Then we can pitch our parent programme at the things they want to know. To do this, the school surveys all parents of pre-school children to find out what they want from the transition programme. We must be doing something right. We have as many parents attending the first session as the last.

At Montmorency South Primary School, an outer suburban school, the transition programme starts early in the second half of the school year. The early years co-ordinator believes it is important to inform parents about the challenges facing children as they commence school and the skills children need to cope with these challenges.

> We have a guest speaker in the middle of the year and we also provide parents with lots of written information about starting school. This helps parents understand that starting school is not just about reading and writing. It's about having the social and emotional skills to cope with the demands of being in a setting that is very different to pre-school. Parents can then make a more informed decision as to whether their child is ready for school or not. Later on parents have opportunities to learn more about how the school operates and how they can help their child start school smoothly. The parent transition programme is part of a much broader parenting programme. One-off events don't work. We provide ongoing parenting courses throughout the early years of school to help parents understand their children's learning and development. Our transition programme is part of this more holistic approach of supporting and involving parents in their children's education. Visits are encouraged between the local pre-schools and the school. These visits are fun and the children feel positive about school right from the start.

The consensus from these schools is that whilst planning comprehensive transition programmes takes time, the programmes are really worthwhile. Staff are familiar with the children and their families. The parents seem more relaxed and less stressed about their children starting school. The children are calmer and the transition to school is more successful.

Overview

Children's adjustment to school is influenced by a multiplicity of factors and in overcoming the discontinuities that have the potential to disrupt children's adjustment to school it is imperative that effective transition programmes are developed so that children are provided with many opportunities to experience the school environment. Parents should be given information about the school. There should be collaboration and the exchange of information between home, pre-school, early childhood services, and schools, and programmes should be responsive to local community values and needs. Transition programme should also include strategies prior to and during the commencement of school.

When transition programmes are carefully and collaboratively planned and effective strategies implemented, the unfamiliar will become familiar, continuity of experiences will be facilitated and the child will feel more secure in the new environment, schools will have valuable knowledge of children's prior experiences, and the speedy adjustment of children and families into the new setting will be facilitated.

References

Ladd, J.M. and Price, J.M. (1987) 'Predicting children's social and school adjustment following the transition from pre-school to kindergarten', *Child Development* 58(5), 1168–89.

Margetts, K. (1997) 'Factors impacting on children's adjustment to the first year of primary school', *Early Childhood Folio 3: A Collection of Recent Research*. NZCER, 53–6

Margetts, K. (2000) 'Indicators of children's adjustment to the first year of schooling'. *Journal for Australian Research in Early Childhood Education* 7(1), 20–30.

Ministerial Review of School-Entry Age in Victoria (MRSEAV) (1992) *The Ministerial Review of School-entry Age in Victoria*. Victoria: Department of School Education.

Chapter 10

Empowering children for transitions

Hilary Fabian

Most children anticipate the start of school with mixed emotions ranging from excitement to apprehension. It is unlikely that all children will respond to starting school in the same way because people react to change in different ways and there are variations in their experiences of the transition. If children settle well in their first year at school it 'sets them up for later' (Laurent, 2000). However, research (Curtis, 1986; Cleave and Brown, 1991; Dowling, 1995; Kienig, 1999) has raised concerns that starting school might cause anxiety that affects children's emotional well-being and their long-term social adjustment, thus hindering future learning. This chapter explores one way of helping children to gain skills of resiliency to help them through the transition from pre-school to school.

Children will find it difficult to envisage what school is like before it has been experienced. Those with older siblings or those who play with pupils from school, may have acquired some understanding of school values and systems vicariously. Within role-play they may have developed 'script knowledge' (Gura, 1996: 37) while they were exploring make-believe school with those who have already had experience of school. However, for the first-born and for many others, school will be a completely new experience. In presenting their picture of school, parents, siblings and friends shape children's thinking, but on arriving at school children may find the reality to be different. If children are to make sense of school with its institutional ways, bewildering new vocabulary and strange culture, most will need support and the opportunity to talk through what school means for them. The way in which children are introduced to their new environment may affect their ability to settle in well. If children can be helped before they start school and during pre-entry visits, to consider what happens there and think about ways they might respond in different situations, they might feel more emotionally secure and ready to meet new challenges with confidence when they begin.

This chapter explores ways of empowering children with skills to cope with transition by using story to address a range of critical incidents and everyday social situations that they will meet at school. It looks at ways of helping children gain an understanding of the nature of school and ways to deal with new situations by encouraging thinking skills (Fisher, 2000: 39) and developing 'emotional literacy' (Goleman, 1998). The chapter argues that by discussing beforehand situations that they might come across in school, and possible approaches, children can begin to gain an understanding of school, develop a greater sense of self-awareness, the motivation to learn, the ability to form relationships, better communication skills and the resourcefulness to meet new challenges.

Into the future

As children approach the end of their pre-school education and the transition to formal schooling, we can empathise with their feelings as they face the unknown. For some there will be few differences but for others the following might arise:

- Many children will have attended a pre-school setting with children of their own age, but they might not have had the opportunity of relating to older children;
- There may be larger numbers of pupils at school. With greater numbers there often comes greater competition. For some children they might not always feel that they succeed as well as before because they are not always able to be the first or the best;
- Children are likely to be faced with different staffing ratios when they start school and have fewer staff than at pre-school. This might mean less interaction with adults than previously;
- Pupils may have less autonomy at school and the curriculum on offer might require them to be less active than previously;
- In this new, often larger, physical environment there might be times of uncertainty about where to go and how to find their way.

When they begin school, there is usually an expectation that children will learn the culture of the classroom and the playground and know the values, traditions, behaviours and beliefs that are characteristic of the class. Children bring their own culture to the class and this may have a different code of conduct to the classroom culture. During the induction to school children will meet some cultural behaviours that they might not have come across before such as having separate toilets for boys and girls, sitting with a large group of children without talking and there might be unfamiliar words, or words used in a different way at school. Learning the culture of school therefore, is

> a complex pursuit of fitting a culture to the needs of its members and of fitting its members and their ways of knowing to the needs of the culture.
> (Bruner, 1996: 43)

The National Curriculum for primary teachers in England (DfEE, 1999) also emphasises the need for children to acquire thinking skills such as information processing, reasoning skills, enquiry skills, creative thinking skills and evaluative skills. These enable children to gain important life skills in a world that is changing at an ever increasing pace and becoming more complex and uncertain.

Skills and 'qualifications' for transition

It would seem, therefore, that at the start of school, children might need skills that equip them for dealing with new situations and that help them to think for themselves. What might these be?

> Although many parents think that success in joining the infant class depends heavily on a child's ability to learn, evidence suggests that personal, rather than intellectual, characteristics have the biggest influence on her chance of having a good start to school.
>
> (Woolfson, 1999: 14)

Fthenakis (1998) indicates that there is a need to teach children to cope with transitions by teaching competencies of resilience. Resilience has been defined as '*normal* development under difficult conditions' (Fonagy *et al.*, 1994: 233). The capacity of children to cope successfully with stress and have the resilience to bounce back and to keep going through difficulties starts with the development of key personal qualities. Krovetz (1999: 7) states that resilient children usually have four attributes in common. These are social competence; problem-solving skills; autonomy; and a sense of purpose and future. Let's explore some of these attributes and others that might be helpful in developing confidence in children.

Social competence

Children grow up in a social world and learn about relationships from interactions with others and the social situations in which they find themselves (Schaffer, 1996). To establish positive relationships with adults and peers they require skills of social understanding. This is to do with the ability to make friends, to enjoy the company of others, to express their own ideas and feelings, to listen to others, to explore across boundaries of associated ideas with others and elicit responses. Starting school with a friend helps with social confidence, but children need knowledge about ways to mix with, and talk to, other children and adults in different situations, and for different purposes. Aggressive children will have difficulties as they will antagonise others and perhaps lose potential friends. Certainly classes function more effectively if children have a sense of community in which they can co-operate, show empathy and concern for one another.

Problem-solving skills

Helping children to work out their own solutions, to investigate and ask questions, empowers them. They can begin to develop a belief in themselves and a 'can do' attitude through hands-on practice. Most parents want to protect their children, so if a problem emerges they often try to solve it without giving the child a chance to discover that s/he has it in his/her power to make a difference. However, independence increases if children are encouraged to develop curiosity, have the opportunity to play around with ideas and plan how to solve it for themselves (Claxton, 2000). This gives them a sense of being in control and will also help them to gain new knowledge.

Self-reliance and determination

Children need the scope to pursue their own approach, to act independently and exert some control over their environment in order to have a sense of their own identity and develop autonomy (Krovetz, 1999). To build up persistence, to think through new possibilities and have the courage to see them through requires a certain amount of risk-taking, while working within their own abilities. Praise and genuine feedback can help children to gain a positive identity. However, too much indiscriminate praise undermines children's love of learning and reduces their creativity, and they might start to deliver the product that they know will be praised. Thus it can undermine children's self-determination, personal resourcefulness, inventiveness and flexibility (Kohn, 1994).

Knowing about not knowing and what to do about it

Gura (1996) proposes that it is a major task for children to make sense of the conventions of social interactions at school. However, children will also need to make sense of a range of other situations and might need help to understand that there will be uncertainties and times when they do not know what to do or where to go. They need to know that it is all right not to know. If they are anxious about their lack of knowledge they can become disruptive or become withdrawn and 'invisible' to a busy teacher. Therefore, children need to be equipped with the ability to face challenges and have the resourcefulness to know what to do in such circumstances. In her keynote speech at the launch of the Research on Thinking and Reasoning conference on 4 May 1999, England's Schools Standards Minister, Estelle Morris said that 'pupils must be taught explicitly to think flexibly and make reasoned judgements'. To do this they need to be encouraged to be inquisitive and to ask questions, to be able to say 'I don't know', but know that they can find out. Strategies for finding out might include knowing who to ask, knowing the words to form a question, developing an awareness of their surroundings, watching others, or playing with ideas to search out meaning. But all these require confidence. The more confident children feel, the more likely they are to tackle the challenges of school life.

Empowerment

Empowerment can support children through the challenges of school. What is meant by empowering children? Empowerment usually refers to having control over the course of one's life and being proactive. Some definitions take into account the environment as well as the individual in that individuals have an understanding of the choices available to them, and choose what they feel is the best course of action. Empowerment can be also seen as a process rather than as an end state (Kieffer, 1984). Kaminski *et al.* (2000: 1359) define empowerment as:

> a developmental process that promotes an active approach to problem solving, increased political understanding, and an increased ability to exercise control in the environment.

They suggest that people progress through a number of stages of a transition and, at each stage, they become more able to analyse issues in context and apply their skills to resolve them successfully. The first stage in this, which Kieffer (1984) calls the 'Era of Entry', is the first step forward from a sense of powerlessness. This is usually caused by a mobilising action that in this case is the imminent start of school. Development can be furthered in the second stage, the 'Era of Advancement', by the help of a mentor and it is this stage that is likely to help children make a successful start to school. Family members, pre-school educators and teachers could be the mentors in this instance who can help children to develop a more analytical understanding of their environment. They can scaffold learning because they are able to identify and nurture potential capabilities, thus helping children to gain skills of recognising situations and dealing with them. Mentors cannot assume that each child brings the same sort of understanding to learning because children each have different past experiences. They need to recognise differences while helping children to construct an understanding of school, develop strategies for approaching new situations, cope with change and solve problems, thereby helping them to gain confidence and the ability to succeed.

Stories

Selwyn (2000) cites work by Rustin and Rustin (1987) that argues that when children are separating from their parents by entering school or joining group cultures, they are particularly interested in story themes of separation, and that these can aid identity-formation. One way of supporting children at the start of school, therefore, might be through stories that focus not only on separation, but also on situations common to most schools. (These might be different in different parts of the world to account for cultural variations.) In these, children could be introduced to a range of ideas relating to a particular theme where they gain a convincing description of the setting, can empathise with the fictional characters and arrive at a conclusion. By incorporating a selection of choices for children to make about the way in which the character (and they) might handle a situation they will be helped to develop self-awareness, decision-making skills and the ability to think through situations in a reasoned way. Mentors can use stories to raise questions with children and form the focus of a discussion about situations that they might encounter at school. Through being given an opportunity to discuss their ideas and interpret the information at hand, children can make their thoughts explicit and reflect on the strategies that they could use to overcome difficulties. McGuinness (1999: 2) suggests that this reflection

> equips pupils to go beyond the information given, to deal systematically yet flexibly with novel problems and situations, to adopt a critical attitude to information and argument as well as to communicate effectively.

By including questions in the stories that ask children to make decisions and discuss why they would choose a particular course of action, children are asked to defend their decisions and consider different points of view. In discussion with the mentor about how they arrived at their decision and why they chose this particular way forward, they can be helped to evaluate the wisdom of their choice of action: They can begin to develop an understanding of the consequences of their actions and decisions, for themselves and for others.

> If children are going to grow more aware of their own values and priorities they ... should be provided with opportunities [to] choose, prize and act, that is: (a) choose freely; (b) choose from alternatives; (c) choose after thoughtful consideration of the consequences of each alternative; (d) cherish and be happy with their choice; (e) be willing to affirm their choice in front of others ...
> (Fisher and Hicks, 1985, cited in Costello, 2000: 32)

The use of story enables a practical approach to help children develop structures in their minds for understanding experiences, think critically about situations, become creative thinkers, able to solve problems and make a difference for the better. As a result they can play a fuller part as a member of the class.

Helping children to think needs imagination on the part of the storyteller or mentor. For example, the mentor might tell a story or draw a cartoon story about a teddy bear or a fictitious child who has just started school and who comes across various situations and 'problems' that need to be solved. The mentor will need to set the scene and adapt the situations to local circumstances, asking the children to help the character to work out the best solution to the problems. By generating ideas and reflecting on outcomes, children can be helped to develop a problem-solving disposition and build confidence to take the risks that might be involved. Working with a group of children, topics could include the following storyboards:

Social competence

Situation: no-one to play with at playtime

Tom has gone outside to play on the playground and, although there are lots of other boys and girls around, he has no one to play with and is feeling lonely. He begins to think of possible solutions by asking himself questions such as:
* Shall I wait for someone to come and play with me?

- Shall I ask some other children if they'd like to join in a game with me?
- Shall I go and say hello to some other children and ask what they're doing?
- Shall I look on the playground and see if there are games painted on the playground so I can play by myself?

Ask the children 'what else could Tom do?' Possible discussion points include safety factors about playing on climbing frames. Some schools have a 'friends' bench where older children act as 'buddies' to those who are on their own. Suggest that children make friends with others who have similar interests, but provide an understanding that not everyone is the same as them. Ask the children:

- What would you choose to do if you were Tom?
- Why would you choose this way?

Further examples of social competence might include stories built around the themes of:

- children working with adults such as classroom assistants;
- children being in groups and expected to listen, answer questions, turn taking in conversations and sharing; being in a large group in a large space for assembly;
- lunch time;
- dealing with bullying.

Solving a problem

Situation: not knowing what to do

Sue is in the classroom and has been given an activity to do that she hasn't seen before and she doesn't know how to do it. She wonders if this is like the one she did last week and begins to ask herself some questions about what to do:

- Shall I kick the chair?
- Shall I ask a friend or the teacher?
- Shall I wait for the teacher to tell me?
- Shall I watch the others for some clues?
- Shall I think about it and have a go?
- What did I do last time?

Ask the children 'what else could Sue do?' Possible discussion points include reassuring children that it's all right not to know. A lot of situations can be confusing and really complicated. In order to build up persistence children need to be encouraged not to give up. A starting point is to say 'I don't know but I'll give it a go' and try different ideas, look for solutions and be inquisitive. Ask the children:

- What would you do if you were Sue?
- Why would you do this?

Further examples of situations where a problem needs solving could include:

- a child having to make a choice between two activities;
- a child deciding what to do if there is no one there to meet them at the end of the day.

The physical environment

Situation: finding the way

Amy wants to go to the toilet. She has asked the teacher if she can go and the teacher has said she may, but she's forgotten the way! She considers what she can do and begins to ponder on some questions:

- Shall I wait for someone to show me?
- Shall I ask the teacher or a friend?
- Shall I set off and look for 'landmarks' along the way?

Ask the children 'what else could Amy do?' A possible focus includes teaching children some key words and phrases that help in asking directions. Some schools have a pairing system of older with younger pupils so children can ask their partner what to do or how to get there. Some children find it useful to practise the route with a friend several times until it becomes familiar. Ask the children:

- Which one would you choose?
- Why choose this one?

A further example of situations in the physical environment might include:

- a child being unable to find his or her coat and bag.

Knowing about not knowing

Situation: not knowing the meaning of a phrase

Sam has been asked to 'line up by the hall door' but he doesn't know what it means. He looks to see if a line has been drawn somewhere but he can't find one. He asks himself what he should do:

- Shall I guess?
- Shall I watch what the others do?
- Shall I just ignore the teacher's instruction?

Ask the children 'what else could Sam do?' Possible discussion points include playing a game to find words/phrases with two or more interpretations. Some words and phrases have hidden meanings such as 'who is sitting beautifully?' At school this often means 'you must sit very still and quietly and listen to the teacher'. Help child to understand that there are often words that people do not understand and they use a dictionary to help them. Ask the children:

- Which one would you choose?
- Why would you choose this solution?

Developing determination

Situation: not good enough!

Jim has tried very hard with his maths but he still doesn't really understand it. He thinks he's no good at maths and thinks:

- I *can* do it! I'm going to concentrate really hard.
- How can I work this out? I'll play around with some ideas.
- I give up. Everyone is better than me.

Ask the children 'what else could Jim do to understand his work? Children may need to be convinced that poor results and difficulties will not last forever but they also need to be given hope, a reason to persevere and the belief in themselves that they can achieve. If adults show distress at their distress this demonstrates that their difficulty is distressing rather than solvable. Ask the children:

- Which one would you choose?
- Why would you choose this one?

Discussion

There are many occasions in which children can prosper without the need for preparation and help. There are also times when choices need to be made between activities that children are keen to do, choices of who to play with, or choices about places to see. Pretend play about school with peers can act as a 'self-help' starting point to extend children's social understanding but they will also need strategies for gaining membership of the group and 'reading' situations that are culturally specific. Children need to be encouraged to have confidence to voice their ideas and need to believe in their ability to think. Children need support and guidance to understand and journey through school successfully. For children to feel confident when they begin school it is helpful if they have developed some skills of resiliency and have:

- a good knowledge of their classroom and some knowledge of the building;

- a knowledge of their teacher and the way s/he thinks;
- an understanding of the language of the school;
- an idea of the nature of the activities that take place in school;
- strategies to make friends;
- a sense of the culture of the classroom.

Stories of critical incidents and commonplace events that occur in everyday life at school can act as a medium to highlight the dominant values espoused by school and some of the situations that children might come across there. Stories create contexts for progress and provide a starting point for discussion that can help children to make sense of themselves, their actions and their environment. However, it is only through living the culture and observing behavioural rituals and norms that school can be fully understood to a point where everyone can operate with shared beliefs and assumptions about 'the way we do things here'.

Using story or pictures can illustrate the situations, but young children find it hard to think hypothetically, to de-contextualise and to use future-tense language. The role of the mentor, therefore, is to explain, to be responsive to a child's needs and sensitive to their moods. They are helping to scaffold the learning and providing a frame for interpreting future situations and relationships. Not only can mentors help children feel connected to school and provide them with strategies to cope with new experiences, but they can also develop a climate of change and raise children's expectations through engaging them in problem-solving situations. This scrutiny of practices may enable children to uncover the hidden assumptions that direct those practices.

Through being philosophically aware and asking questions, mentors can encourage children in their thinking. The initial questions in each of the above scenarios are to do with enquiry and information-processing skills. These are questions that ask: What do I need to find out? What do I need to know? What questions do I need to ask? (Fisher, 2000: 39). The questions that ask about what else can be done and question why a particular route has been chosen, refer to reasoning, creative thinking and evaluation skills. These are guided by questions such as: What's my reason for this? Is there another possible answer? What do I think about the issue? The group discussion serves to give children other choices as well as indicating that not everyone sees life in the same way. It helps children to have a respect for others' points of view, the courage to defend their own point of view, the confidence to question or challenge any given idea, and the willingness to be open to changing their opinions (Fisher, 2000). It also helps children to gain the language of discourse about these matters. Work by Befrienders International uses stories in conjunction with discussion to help young children explore their emotions concerning difficult situations. It has indicated that there is a marked improvement in children's social skills, empathy and assertiveness as a result of using stories.

Through stories of critical incidents and everyday situations that happen in school followed by a discussion of various solutions, children can be helped to interpret and make sense of their experiences, and begin to understand the taken-for-granted assumptions and beliefs of the school culture. They can explore the separation from home, the possibility for new relationships, ways to approach situations and develop a determination to succeed. By being 'choosers' (Claxton, 2000) and through making decisions, children begin to make sense of their own identity, construct their own values and learn how to direct their lives. These choices can be rehearsed through the scenarios, resulting in feelings of accomplishment. By having opportunities to deal with the school culture, children can construct their own realities and meanings then adapt them to the system. Having experience of a range of possible situations is likely to help children develop, but the reality of school will not occur until children begin school and they gain continuous first-hand experience of the culture. However, by discussing possible solutions, and rehearsing strategies for dealing with eventualities beforehand, children can be helped to cope with unfamiliar situations and step into the unknown with confidence.

References

Bruner, J.S. (1996) *The Culture of Education.* Cambridge, MA: Harvard University Press.

Claxton, G. (2000) 'A sure start for an uncertain world', *Early Education* 30, Spring. Four page insert.

Cleave, S. and Brown, S. (1991) *Early To School: Four Year Olds in Infant Classes.* London: NFER/Routledge.

Costello, P.J.M. (2000) *Thinking Skills and Early Childhood Education.* London: David Fulton.

Curtis, A.M. (1986) *A Curriculum for the Pre-school Child.* London: NFER-Nelson.

Department for Education and Employment (1999) *The National Curriculum: Handbook for Primary Teachers in England.* London: QCA.

Dowling, M. (1995) *Starting School at Four: A Joint Endeavour.* London: Paul Chapman Publishing.

Fisher, R. (2000) 'Philosophy for children: teaching thinking and values'. In Fisher, R. (ed.) *Connected Thinking.* Manchester: Society for Education Officers.

Fisher, S. and Hicks, D. (1985) *World Studies 8–13: A Teacher's Handbook.* Edinburgh: Oliver and Boyd.

Fonagy, P., Steele, M., Steele, H., Higgit, A. and Target, M. (1994) 'The theory and practice of resilience', *Journal of Child Psychology and Psychiatry* 35(2), 231–57.

Fthenakis, W.E. (1998) 'Family transitions and quality in early childhood education', *European Early Childhood Education Research Journal* 6(1), 5–17.

Goleman, D. (1998) *Working with Emotional Intelligence.* London: Bloomsbury

Gura, P. (1996) 'Roles and relationships'. In Robson, S. and Smedley, S. (eds), *Education in Early Childhood.* London: David Fulton Publishers.

Kaminski, M., Kaufman, J.S., Graubarth, R. and Robins, T.G. (2000) 'How do people become empowered? A case study of union activists', *Human Relations* 53(10), October, 1357–83.

Kieffer, C.H. (1984) 'Citizen empowerment: a developmental perspective'. In Rappaport, J. and Hess, R. (eds), *Studies in Empowerment: Steps Toward Understanding and Action.* New York: Haworth.

Kienig, A. (1999) 'Adjustment to new settings in the early years: how to help children with this transition'. Paper presented at 9th European Conference on Quality in Early Childhood Education. Helsinki.

Kohn, A. (1994) 'The risks of rewards', *ERIC Digest*, 1–2 Urbana, IL: ERIC.

Krovetz, M.L. (1999) *Fostering Resiliency*. California: Corwin Press.

Laurent, C. (2000) 'The real life class', *Guardian Education* Tuesday 11 April, 6–7.

McGuinness, C. (1999) *From Thinking Skills to Thinking Classrooms: A Review and Evaluation of Approaches for Developing Pupils' Thinking*. Research Report No 115 commissioned by the Department for Education and Employment. Norwich: HMSO.

Rustin, M. and Rustin, M. (1987) *Narratives of Love and Loss*. London: Verso.

Schaffer, H.R. (1996) *Social Development*. Oxford: Blackwell.

Selwyn, J. (2000) 'Technologies and environments: new freedoms, new constraints'. In Boushel, M. Fawcett, M. and Selwyn, J. (eds), *Focus on Early Childhood: Principles and Realities*. Oxford: Blackwell Science.

Woolfson, R. (1999) 'Be prepared', *Nursery World* 99(3662), 14–15.

Chapter 11

Transitions without school

Jan Fortune-Wood

Intrinsically motivated transitions

The notion of transition implies that there is some destination that is being aimed for. In the school setting the destination is a pre-ordained one. It is certainly one that educationalists, politicians, teachers, parents or some combination thereof believe to be in the child's best interests. It is almost certainly a destination that will have at its core such goals as self-reliance, autonomy, the development of problem-solving skills and socialisation. Despite this, when we speak of transitions in the school setting we are talking about coerced transitions. However sensitively handled and whatever mechanisms we put in place to assist children to manage, the transition is externally motivated and its goals are circumscribed by the artificial boundaries of the institution.

In the school setting, whilst we want children to have a certain ability to be self-reliant, resourceful individuals, we also want to ensure that they are not so self-reliant that they question the curriculum or the basic structure of school relationships. Within schools, we may speak highly of independent thought and action, but that does not mean that children can expect to be the architects of their own tailor-made education or that they can autonomously decide when and whether to attend particular classes. We will certainly value problem-solving skills, but the problems will be those presented by an artificially constructed institution and the solutions found must always remain within a very tight framework. Similarly the socialisation that we ask children to undertake is unique to the school environment. At no other stage of life are children likely to be in large groups of people of exactly the same age, in a mandatory environment, being directed by a single individual to perform tasks they have not chosen. The artificial nature of the peer group, based on age, not interest, is a poor pre-cursor to adult social interaction, especially as the work place moves away from the factory model towards increasingly post-modern and disparate models.

Not all children, however, make this transition. An increasing number of children are home educated and their transitions occur within their daily lives. Some of these children will have attended school for some time and will, therefore, have experience of school-based transitions. Others will have no school-based experience at any point during their education. What the majority of home-educated children will have in common, whether they have periods in school or not, is the experience of encountering and managing intrinsically motivated transitions. Families choose home education for a wide variety of reasons, but in many cases the children, even at very young ages are active participants in this choice. The child who has attended school for some time will need the skills to consider how the change will effect any established friendships, how new social contacts can be made and how to begin to perceive education in a totally new framework. Particularly, though not exclusively, for a child whose education at home is not formally structured, but follows a child-led, autonomous route, there will be considerations of the boundaries and mergers between life and learning. These are major transitional issues and ones which home-educating parents find their children make smoothly and adeptly.

Two particular factors play an important role in the smoothness of transitions made by home-educated children. The children are aided by having one key environment (the home) as the base for their learning, even though it is highly likely that they will also use many outside environments to augment the learning process. Second, the children have only a limited number of key adults to relate to as assistants in their learning (most often parents, grandparents and occasional tutors employed by family) and this generally means that there is no split of expectation and educational philosophy between teacher and parent; home and school.

For some home-educated children transitions back into school for specific periods or for specific ends may be part of the experience of transitions. Some children, for example will use school to complete examination courses (though of course many families negotiate exams totally outside the school system). Of course, many home-educated children will never experience transitions in their lives that are in any way connected with school. Is this a cost or benefit of home education? Does this mean that home-educated children fail to develop the means to cope with transitions and become overly dependent on their parents, lacking in self identity and autonomy, less able to cope with unfamiliar and stressful situations and less socially adept? Are home-educated children unlikely either to be able to cope with life transitions or exist in environments that offer no challenge and stimulus?

It is my contention that the learning gained from making self-determined transitions out of, or into the school environment and the learning gained in an environment where there are no school based transitions affords a considerable benefit to home-educated children. Far from being hindered by this different state of transitions, I want to argue that home education provides an excellent opportunity for children to develop the transition skills which are most appropriate to their individual contexts, needs and motivation.

Self reliance or apron strings?

The ability to make transitions is a basic human trait. As we grow we develop a sense of our own identity and an increased reliance on our own abilities. The imposition of school into the lives of young children marks an artificial boundary which demands that development has reached particular key markers, whether the individual is intrinsically motivated to have reached them or not. Children entering school need to know how to use the toilet alone, how to manipulate cutlery and eat relatively quickly and quietly, how to dress and undress with some speed, how to wait their turn in conversation, how to negotiate their way through a day without the advice or input of the adults who they have come to know and trust. None of these skills in themselves are bad things. They are all things that one would expect to see in any growing child (barring particular special needs), but when they are suddenly imposed at the age of four or six, some children will find that they are simply not at that stage of development and these children may become labelled as 'immature' and soon find themselves in a spiral of not coping and facing failure.

Not being ready to make school-based transitions at a particular time can have detrimental effects on future learning and self-esteem. Although institutions attempt to be responsive in varying degrees, it tends to be the case that it is the child who is not ready who is perceived as having or being the problem, rather than the structure. Home education turns this around and enables critical questions to be posed whilst also allowing the individual child to make fluid, self-directed transitions. Helping children to adjust might certainly be a worthy pursuit, but the underlying assumption is that the environment being adjusted to is normative and represents an objective, rational standard of behaviour and outcomes. Home education allows that this may not be the case and opens up the question of radical educational diversity.

Home-educated children make the same life transitions through phases of development as school going children, but they do so at a speed and in an order which is highly individual and which carries no risk of being seen as failing. This can bring with it the suspicion that home-educated children are over protected, insulated from the demands of the world in ways that will ultimately do them no service and liable to be less mature, more shy and less skilled than their school going peers. This is not the case. What emerges is not a picture of retiring children tied to their mother's apron strings, but of a wider range of individuals, some of whom will develop certain skills and confidence rather earlier than school children, whilst developing other skills much later. There is no reason why these children should not make the same developmental strides. The picture that emerges may look more idiosyncratic to the outside eye. One might, for example encounter a home-educated child aged six who cannot tie her shoe laces and still needs assistance with the toilet, but who can competently and safely boil an egg and who can go to the local shop herself, negotiate a purchase and handle the change. The skills not yet developed carry no stigma since there is no peer pressure and no risk that the child's individual pace is going to compromise the functionality of the environment. Rather, skills will simply follow on according to the child's intrinsic motivation. The child, without the pressure of externally motivated transitions, has a full sense of control over his life and environment and is likely to be more confident in facing new transitions as they arise naturally.

I invited a group of home-educating parents to comment on their perceptions of transitions without school and got consistent answers despite differences of life style and educational philosophy. I asked about children's willingness to make transitions for themselves, such as being willing to stay home alone, use local shops, take charge of their learning etc.

> I do not have much to do when they are working, as they tend to ask each other for help, and puzzle out a difficulty between them …

> They come up with their own project ideas and insist on doing it themselves – learning from trial and error. They also instigate trips to the library and choose their own books.

> After a while out of school my child is planning for the future and has realistic ideas about life. She can see the need for a transition in the next few years and is no longer reluctant to grow up.

This sense of control and self-determination often arises from the basic decision to home educate itself, since the decision is almost invariably one in which the child participates and often has the casting choice. Children, who know, from a very young age, that they have this measure of choice and control over such a major part of their lives as education, are unlikely to be children who feel alienated, over-protected or self doubting.

This is not to say that protection is never a motivation, or at least a part of the motivation for home education. Some parents choose home education to protect their children from particular influences at school, which they believe to be detrimental. They might be families who want to follow a particular religious faith or families who want to live one of a range of alternative lifestyles. Other parents come to home education for very overt reasons of protection, where a child has been severely bullied or where a child's particular individuality is clearly at odds with the needs of an institutional environment. Even in these cases, there is no need to fear that the children will be immature, incapable individuals.

In my questions to home-educating parents I asked how home-educated children learn self-reliance and avoid being over-protected.

> My children have learned that Mum is a busy person. They will often get their own breakfast, and bring me their laundry without my having to ask. They volunteer to help neighbours with garden work. They initiate play with unknown children when we are out. I believe that the self confidence they have learned as home-educated children is the reason my once shy children are now socially confident.

Mine are certainly not tied to my apron strings. They go out on their own to the shops, library and friends' houses. They are more confident than they were when they were at school, particularly when dealing with adults.

We tend to assume that being thrown into the lions' den is character forming and whilst this may be how adults often think of their own experiences retrospectively it could be equally true that being subjected to certain experiences (whether at all or simply at the wrong point for a particular individual) can be character damaging. We tend to make many assumptions about the things that parents should protect their children from, whilst also assuming that they are in error if they attempt to protect their children from experiences which have become seen as 'normal' through the experience of mass schooling. Home education questions some of these assumptions. Home education allows parents and children to find highly individual solutions to acquiring life skills and making developmental transitions, without age prescribed timetables for so doing. By providing a model of transitions that is based on intrinsic motivation or family pattern, home education proposes not that we foster a generation of children who are immature, skills poor or mollycoddled, but rather children who become self-reliant and innovative at their own pace. Furthermore, the model of intrinsically motivated transitions ensures that the prospect of failure is almost negligible. The range of ages at which home-educated children make any given transition may cover a much wider age spread, but very few home-educated children are going to feel as though they are failures with no prospects, or label themselves abnormal at the age of seven or eight.

An assumption of autonomy

The transition model of schools, with its stress on acquiring a range of key skills shortly prior to, and very quickly after, entering the school environment, regardless of personal development, is a model in which autonomy is a goal to be achieved by the end of the educational experience. For many home-educators, however, autonomy is an assumption that is made from infancy and which underpins the whole alternate educational experience. This is seen most clearly in the proponents of the 'taking children seriously' (TCS) educational philosophy, though it is present in various degrees of the home-educating community.

> TCS philosophy maintains that coercion is detrimental to rational thinking and therefore damaging to education ...
> Once the premise is accepted that coercion causes damaged thinking, education and life can never be the same again ... it demands a different model for problem solving and learning: a consensual, rational model in which everyone's ideas are equally valued, everyone's ideas are equally valued, everyone's human fallibility is equally recognised, and everyone's autonomy is equally respected.
>
> (Fortune-Wood, 2000b: 1 and 3)

For many home-educators and particularly for those who subscribe to the TCS philosophy, autonomy is not a desired outcome, but a human property to be respected and valued all the way through the educational process. In this sense there is no transition or series of transitions to personal autonomy within an educational framework, but rather a model in which parents act as trusted advisors as children explore their own autonomy throughout life.

With this assumption of autonomy, education becomes something which children choose and design, with as much input as they want from parents and other trusted advisors. Moreover, the traditional demarcations between what does or does not constitute education often become increasingly blurred, with time spent gazing at the ceiling, playing computer games, engaging in play and watching general TV programmes taking their place alongside reading and subject based material as equally valid forms of learning.

With such an extensive control over the content and style of education and life, home-educated children can begin from a basic presumption of their own autonomy and can develop that autonomy at their own pace according to their intrinsic motivation. Most importantly, home-educated children can experience life transitions not as abrupt, externally imposed expectations that will divide them into winners or losers, but as natural events that occur by consent and pose no threat. This gives home-educated children an increased opportunity to experience control and success. Furthermore it sets up positive patterns of thinking about change and transition.

I enquired of home-educating parents how home-educated children develop their own sense of identity and autonomy when they are based in the home environment.

> I need my own space sometimes and appreciate that the children also need space from me, their father, each other and the house. They have joint and separate friends, activities they do on their own and their own rooms and responsibilities.

> In the early years of home-educating my now grown-up children, I heard a lot about how they couldn't be self-reliant, that they would be shy and unable to get along with their peers etc. ... nothing could be further from the truth.

Many school-going children experience a considerable degree of autonomy in their infancy and, sometimes on through their early years education. These children, though adept in many ways, can find the transition to school enormously difficult because they move out of this environment of autonomy into one of conformity, lack of choice and paucity of explanation. Within schools there are a range of solutions sought for this experience of discontinuity and children are assisted in making adjustments. However, only home education fundamentally questions whether this adjustment is necessary or truly in the child's best interest. Home-educated children, like all children, benefit from knowledge of varied environments and their constraints and demands, but learning about these environments and how to participate in them does not require being forced to enter a compulsory environment at a young age.

Children in school may be enticed to surrender their autonomy for a perceived benefit, namely that they gain valuable learning. However home-educated children are aware that they can have both learning and autonomy, that they can satisfy their intrinsic educational goals without having to endure enforced transitions or loss of autonomy. Whilst educationalists can make helpful suggestions about assisting school children through transitions, home-educated children have the advantage of already being in learning environments that are individualised and responsive; of already enjoying a stable social network from which to develop new social skills.

Coping with the unfamiliar

It is perhaps not an unfair question to wonder how home-educated children, especially those who experience an autonomous style of education, are prepared for those transitions which occur without warning and over which we might have little or no control. Life is not, after all, predictable and it might be argued that school children, who have had to face transitions not of their choosing and quickly acquire the skills to negotiate them successfully, will be much better served when it comes to facing a real world where people die unexpectedly, families break up, employment is not guaranteed etc.

First it must be noted that not all children who go to school do come through the experience of enforced transitions successfully. Some children fail at the first hurdle and go through their school life alienated and confused; socially, culturally and academically at odds with the school environment. Many children leave school with poor problem solving skills, low resilience to stress and unfamiliar situations and an inability to cope rationally with difficult conditions. Going to school is not a guarantee of acquiring the skills that go with making healthy life transitions, but even assuming that we compare home-educated children with those most successful at meeting the challenges of school based transitions, there is still no need to fear that home education is a detriment.

> Conventional parents sometimes object that removing boundaries simply gives children a false notion of what the world is like. They insist that we need to experience a certain level of frustration, hardship and suffering in order to survive in the real world. It must always be remembered that we all live in the real world. Our circumstances may differ dramatically, but there is still only one world in which we can live. Living well in it is not 'unreal' …
>
> … Life contains enough risks and enough learning opportunities for children to see for themselves that bad things happen. They can learn how to tackle

and handle the real tragedies and complex problems by having lots of access to information and good models of how to problem solve creatively. We do not prepare for a journey to a famine stricken country by starving ourselves, but by building up our strength and learning all we can about basic nutrition and survival. There is not intrinsic value in being in a state of distress. It serves only to crush our ability to think rationally.

(Fortune-Wood, 2000: 83–4)

Home education often suffers from an overly quaint image of insular, traditional families gathered around the kitchen table to learn carefully selected material under the protective eye of 'Mum', who acts as a screen from the real world. In fact, there is no singular image or stereotype to offer. The rapidly expanding home-educating community is extremely diverse. Home education is perhaps better described as 'home-based education', with community facilities, libraries, museums, cinemas, theatres, internet communication and much more providing a whole plethora of windows onto the world. Similarly there is no one family style amongst home-educators. Rather it is a movement that includes families from every religion and social class, and encompasses nuclear families, communities, single parents and gay families. Within this vast cross section of society, children learn to cope with the real transitions that arise in their real homes and communities. They may be protected from artificially imposed transitions, but this need not make them less capable of coping with what life throws at them. In fact, it can be argued, that being accustomed to success and having a model of problem-solving that makes them feel in control of all those areas that can be controlled is likely to promote positive, rational thinking and render them more flexible and open minded, more accustomed to having to employ their own personal resources.

Perhaps even more note worthy is that Rothermel noted that home education itself is often the catalyst of transition for a family,

> Often following commencement of home-education, a shift in family convention occurred. Most notable was 'loss' of one income. Parents often altered their working patterns to accommodate the children's learning and within many families both parents worked part time. Parents also regularly took to studying. The research found that for many, the onset of home-education led a previously conventional family to radically alter their perspective on life and education.
>
> (Rothermel, 2000)

In other words, it is common for home-educating families to evolve a pattern of transition together, which may well provide a secure model for future life transitions. By taking charge of their education or at least having a much greater input than they could expect at school, home-educated children are well used to problem solving. Similarly home-educated children are a constant part of family life and decision making often by virtue of simply being at home full time. This in turn engenders maturity and resilience. Home-educated children have plenty of experience of coping with stressful or difficult situations; the difference is that these situations are not artificially contrived or imposed by an external institution.

It is conceivable that the experience of not going through enforced, early transitions, far from being detrimental to the ability to cope with later transitions, actually assists in forming coping mechanisms. Similarly, building strong family bonds could later prove helpful to the social networking that is essential to surviving ongoing life transitions, such as marriage, deaths etc.

This is backed up by the responses of home-educating parents to the question of how home-educated children deal with unfamiliar of difficult circumstances or sudden, unpredictable changes in their lives:

> School doesn't teach change and transition. It teaches you to be one of the many, herded through the system like the rest of the sheep. Being home-educated does not mean you cut yourself off from the rest of the world and remain in isolation. There are still changes and transitions ... Everyone comes across unfamiliar and difficult circumstances once in a while have the love and support of their families to help them twenty four hours a day, seven days a week.

A family who had experienced the death of a child, wrote:

> I believe our experience has been one of 'togetherness' for want of a better word, and respecting each child's integrity, whilst working hard at our relation-ships, being honest about our feelings, and making friends of quality rather than quantity. This has helped each child make each transition with less trauma than might have been expected ... We have had enormous amounts of time to deal with the really important things of life and death, and sums etc. can wait.

Socialisation

There is a fear that home-educated children lose out socially and that, in not making school-based transitions, they miss out on key social development. This is a misconception and home-educating parents report that far from being a detriment, home based education has an enormously positive influence on the socialisation process.

> The theory that ... home-educated children are more likely to be socially incompetent is one based on prejudice or on untested and entrenched assump-tions. There is still a commonly held notion that children must learn to 'socialise' in large groups within even larger institutions in order to fit them for society. This is largely based on a failure to question why schools are organised in this way. School organisation reflects a societal organisation that was more prevalent at the Industrial Revolution, fitting children for conformity in factory work and other large-scale organisation, but whilst

schools have largely maintained this once 'appropriate' structure society has moved on.

(Fortune-Wood, 2000a: 60)

A wide range of research findings backs up these anecdotal reports of home-educating parents (cf. Thomas, 1998; Meighan, 1997). Rothermel has recently pointed out that regardless of socio-economic background, gender or educational attainment levels of parents, home-educated children not only achieved academically, but also demonstrated good social skills (Rothermel 2000).

What home-educated children 'miss out' on is not socialisation *per se*, but rather on enforced socialisation and the coercive peer pressure and bullying that are too often by-products of school socialisation. As Roland Meighan has noted,

> ... Home-schooling families actually create a much higher quality of social life in their practice of family-centred education, in three ways. First of all they use the home as a springboard into the community using libraries, museums, places of interest in both town and country. In the process they rub shoulders with people of all ages. ... Secondly, they locate and join groups such as Scouts, Guides, and Woodcraft Folk, as well as groups or classes in judo, swimming and other sports, or natural history and other pursuits. Thirdly, they seek out other home-schooling families and do things in co-operation.
>
> (Meighan, 1999)

There is no reason why home-educated children should not make strong social bonds along with smooth and intrinsically motivated transitions into their own sense of independence and self reliance.

Conclusions

Home-educators come from every lifestyle and a diverse range of educational philosophies. Despite this diversity there is a consensus that not being involved in school-based transitions is not only not to children's detriment, but beneficial. The work of Rothermel in surveying home-educators has substantively shown that neither academic progress nor social skills are hampered, but are rather assisted (Rothermel, 2000). The work of Webb has highlighted the ability of home-educated young people to move from home education into a wide diversity of adult education and occupations (Webb, 1999). Home-educating parents similarly report that their children develop the skills of transition very smoothly.

Transitions are part of life and normal social engagement. During the course of life, some of these transitions will involve individuals moving out of the family into institutions of varying nature and it might be argued that this alone will give school-going children an advantage over their home-educated peers. However, it must be remembered that prison aside, no other institution that an individual enters will be compulsory. Home-educated children have just as much experience of the transitions of birth, death, puberty, leaving home, marriage etc. Furthermore, home education is rarely pursued around the kitchen table to the exclusion of the community. Most home-educated children are adept from a young age at using a wide variety of community facilities and move between different environments with differing demands with ease. They may not have any sharp lines of demarcation between learning and not learning; education and life, particularly if they are used to an autonomous style of home-education, but this is no hindrance in assessing and responding to different environments. Additionally, home-educated children, who are used to managing their learning and time may very well be ideally placed to take up work opportunities in a post modern society. Home-educated young people find that challenge and difficulty can be engaged in without extrinsic motivation and an environment of success, responsiveness and autonomy can be an excellent base from which to face unexpected circumstances.

The notion of transition implies that there is some destination that is being aimed for. For home-educated children this destination is much more open-ended both in form and time scale. It also involves a great deal more autonomy and self-direction. None-the-less, without the experience of school as providing an early and ongoing model of transition, home-educated children experience a wide range of transition experiences. They can move between environments, develop self-reliance, independence and a sense of their own identities. They form relationships and on average, are socially skilful. In short, without outcomes being required of them and without having a pre-defined model of transition, home-educated children none-the-less make a complex range of transitions.

References

Fortune-Wood, J. (2000a) *Doing It Their Way*. Nottingham: Educational Heretics Press.

Fortune-Wood, J. (2000b) *Without Boundaries*. Nottingham: Educational Heretics Press.

Meighan, R. (1999) 'A superstition called socialisation'. Educational Heretics Website, www.gn.apc.org. (A version of this also appeared in *Natural Parent* Magazine, Nov/Dec 1998.)

Meighan, R. (1997) *The Next Learning System: And Why Home-schoolers are Trailblazers*. Nottingham: Educational Heretics Press.

Rothermel, P. (2000) 'Home-education: a critical evaluation'. Unpublished paper presented at the British Psychological Society Annual Education Conference, University of Exeter.

Thomas, A. (1998) *Educating Children At Home*. London: Cassell.

Webb, J. (1999) *Those Unschooled Minds: Home-educated Children Grow Up*. Nottingham: Educational Heretics Press.

Chapter 12

Conclusions
Debating transitions, continuity and progression in the early years

Aline-Wendy Dunlop and Hilary Fabian

In this final chapter we set out to debate continuity and progression in transitions in the early years. Although we will argue a certain universality of childhood and have identified common issues amongst the authors, we find we have to revisit and re-present the themes introduced, through our conceptual framework for transition, a little differently as a result of this debate. Although there are commonalities in the transition experiences presented, there are also particularities: a shared language to describe transitions may not be a mutual one. There are in fact a variety of discourses of transition held and researched: these too will be debated. In this way we will draw together the various strands that emerge from the chapters and attempt to link research, theory and practice. We will also present a model which will reflect the possible agency of children in the transition process, and attempt to show the importance of the child's agency in the interrelatedness of the ecological systems approach which has been informative for all of us. We then go on to ask what shall we do now?

We look at how society frames and conceptualises childhood, how teachers, families and community each entertain constructs of childhood, children as entrants to early years settings, and as primary school novices. Thus the debate must include a reflection on the day-to-day experiences of children: what Dalli calls their 'lived lives' and the various discourses held by parents and pre-school and primary educators, and which influence children. These multiple discourses offer a collective appreciation of the condition of childhood in transition: educational, familial and personal transition.

We reflect on what can be learned from home educators that has direct implications for the institutionalised systems of which most children are a part. Institutions which were often designed for a different world, a world which held different views of childhood and which was perhaps less interested in the voice of the child than we are now. An interest which is however also debateable as we see the rise of the assertion of children's rights matched conversely by a renewed institutional structuring of childhood (James *et al.*, 1998).

Given that the socio-cultural contexts in which children live vary considerably, and even within classrooms will not be homogenous, we assert that concepts of childhood are not constant, they are embedded in social, political, philosophical, psychological and economic understandings. Each of these disciplines may oblige certain conceptions of childhood, childhood which we find can be both a private experience of families and a political symbol for change. Early childhood can thus be seen as an instrumental tool in which governments invest for their national futures: what Jenks (1996: 15) calls the 'promise' of childhood, rather than the present. Such a promise is implicit in current social inclusion and child poverty policies in the UK, as well as being part of UK interventions into early learning (HMI, 2001): interventions which have strongly affected children's transition experiences in recent years in the UK. Whilst well-intentioned and important, such initiatives can also be read as social control.

The exercise of adult or institutional power can affect children in different ways. Indeed it can be argued that parents of primary aged children, and in our view pre-school too, in exercising power over them at home, are also pleased to promote competence and independence in terms of self-care (Mayall, 1994). In schools children's competence can be diminished by the demands of curriculums. It is essential that we consider appropriate pedagogies which allow children to be children, and not always be part of the chase for adulthood – always becoming and never being (James *et al.*, 1998). Each of the authors have experienced a development of curriculum guidance in some form in recent years in their countries.

The intention claimed for these initiatives is to ensure quality of early childhood experiences: we have to question if through this laudable aim, we are in fact minimising differences, reducing agency and promoting a universal child. If we constantly strive for what society wants children to become, what developmental psychology expects, we may render the child herself incomplete. Identity and roles will change for young children in educational transitions. Can this be done without disharmony and dissonance? If we can think of the child as a social actor (Dalli, Griebel and Niesel, Fabian and Dunlop) then educational systems do not need to approach them from the perspective of 'an assumed shortfall of competence, reason or significance' (James *et al.*, 1998: 207).

This then calls for an exploration of the ways in which the schooling process and children's induction into it intersects with home and the community to structure or support the learning experiences of children (Pollard and Filer, 1996). The overlaps and interconnectedness, the potential for parent influence and contribution (Johansson) and the role of the pre-school as an arena for learning and social development which supports and prepares the child and the parent for school, must be coupled with change in the institutional approaches.

As we look critically at educational transitions in childhood we are faced with a need to define what we understand by 'childhood', whose childhood it is, who 'we' are, who 'children' are and whose 'land' it is (Burman, 1994) – is it transitional territory between pre-school and school in which families have a part and can be social actors and agents in the transition process – or should we look for difference and disjunction and support children through rites of passage (Van Gennep, 1960) – children becoming, waiting to be processed, moving on to the next stage. If we embrace the idea of co-construction, then the co-construction of transition must be shared by all the actors: teachers, parents and children in the context of their own particular community, but not bound by it. (Johansson).

We need to move beyond contextualisation to exploration. Here we propose that transition, continuity and progression are key elements in school success. Transition being the passage from one place, stage, state, style or subject to another over time. The intense and accelerated developmental demands which children encounter needs to be matched by changes which are continuous rather than abrupt, where connections are emphasised and the time sequence is uninterrupted. Discontinuity occurs for children when experience is intermittent and separated by time and by space. Progression implies an onward motion, an advance, an integration of the previous into the present. Changes of relationships, space, time, contexts for learning, and demands of learning itself, combine at moments of transition. If on the other hand transition is conceived of as a process, with attention paid to giving children the opportunity to acquire the knowledge they need of situation, people, timings, expectations (Fabian), then children might have the chance to predict events and feel some control.

> This detailed awareness of the definition of the situation and its power to dictate appropriate behaviour may well be associated with the fact that school children experience frequent and regular changes of situation over which they have little control. They must pay close attention to the requirements of any one situation such that within its own terms it becomes predictable. Once a situation becomes predictable then competent appropriate behaviour becomes possible.
>
> (Davies, 1982: 113)

We have argued the importance of a sense of competence, of the need for children to have the tools with which to 'read' the situation and the teacher. Children in our studies have been found to be creative, fluent and capable, and often to experience a loss of that confidence in the initial days and weeks of school. If this was unavoidable the thesis of our book would be different. But it is avoidable. Children need to be able to be agents in their own transitions, rather than undermined through change. The embarrassment of children when they can't read the situation or find recognisable clues is something as adults we may fail to consider fully.

As we reflect back on the research and practice experiences of the authors, common issues are raised, as well as differing experiences and views. How transitions themselves are viewed is such an interesting area of debate. Different groupings could be identified: a cluster of authors who focus on the need to support children in transition, a group who consider that a greater mutuality of view between educators in early years pre-school settings and early years elementary school settings would result in schools being more ready for children (Bröstrom and Peters), rather then a strong need to prepare children for change. Herein rests an important debate: transition from home to pre-school and on to school may be just a foretaste of later transitions. If this is so, the developmental disharmonies and their successful passage will equip children to be more resilient in future since contemporary life will demand a range of social, familial and institutional changes and integration (Fthenakis, 1998). Implicit in such a view might be the assumption that the destination being aimed for is 'how it should be', and that it is only the individual who needs to change.

Such an assumption needs to be challenged, and often is by the authors in this book. Given that differences in settings remain manifest in the early years, children will need support to anticipate change, to embrace it confidently and to enjoy what the new setting offers. However the assumption that children should be empowered to cope should not exclude the opportunity that exists for the various settings and people involved to work together in greater harmony. To get to know each other, and to debate and discuss the differences in the experiences offered in order to weigh up what is in the best interests of the children concerned, is a valid aim for which school managers need to plan. Part of our argument has also been the importance of asking children. Much of the research which exists into children's culture has taken place in schools. As can be seen by Griebel and Niesel's work educational ethnographies provide insights into the social worlds of children (Pollard, 1985). At the same time the very institutions being explored as contexts for understanding children's perspectives are themselves pre-structuring childhood. The adult world through which childhood is defined includes family and home, school and educational systems. Our research embraces home and school, community and wider society, our conceptual model of transition is a nested one, but not constant.

Presented as a systems approach on an ecological model, our conceptual framework is transformed, and our contention that children, teachers and parents might co-construct transitions can be seen in context. When Bronfenbrenner (1989) argued the importance of studying development in context, he envisaged nested and interrelated ecological systems on a number of levels. It is essential to recognise that the people occupying each level and each system are also active, by their inter-connections, in how each system is experienced (Dunlop, 2002b). Each level is related to and influenced by the others with the micro systems of day-to-day experience at the core, and the other levels successively embracing the more central day-to-day levels. The child in educational transitions occupies three environments or microsystems: their home world, the pre-school world and the school world. Although each contains the developing person, we need to look beyond the single settings to the relationships between them. These interconnections can be seen as important for the child as events taking place within any one of the single settings: Bronfenbrenner (1979) calls them mesosystems.

A further level will house initiatives and events at which the transition child may not even be present. Despite the fact that local educational policies, programmes, social services, health care, housing issues, parental employment, interventions, the local community's facilities and the reorganisation of any one of these elements may not be experienced by the child at first hand, all may profoundly affect the child at their centre. We have included 'working together' and 'information' as critically important elements here: elements which empower child, parent and teacher. Further there may be various discourses of childhood

(Burman, 1994) and several cultures represented (Bronfenbrenner, 1979). These discourses and cultures may be distinctly different and so there may be a pressing need to cross over them, to develop a shared language and a mutual view of any particular child.

Beyond these relatively local influences, a fourth and all encompassing layer can be envisaged: the macrosystem. Here the theoretical conception is that wider influences, beyond the determination of the child, the family or the educators will exert strongly felt influences on the day-to-day. These wider influences include government policy, the effects of social and political institutions, the significance of the wider culture, the ideologies and social values held, and the rights and responsibilities of society as a whole. These environments extend beyond the behaviour of individuals and the immediate situation encompassed, but nevertheless have immediate significances (see Figure 12.1).

If the effective functioning of each part of the system is seen to depend on the interconnections between them, then joint participation, communication, working together and the sharing of information in each setting about the others, are each going to be vital for successful transitions within and between settings. Questions are then demanded of these various settings, for example, does the child enter a new situation such as school alone or in the company of familiar friends, peers or adults? Is the child and family provided with any information about or experience in the new setting before actual entry is made? What is the nature of this information and its delivery: participatory or distanced? What is the nature of the experience in the new setting: is it a visit, or actual participation with children who already know the system? Once prior knowledge is acquired, how does such knowledge affect the subsequent course of behaviour in the new setting? Ecological transitions bring shifts in role, or setting, or identity, or curriculum. The process of becoming a pre-school child or a schoolchild may have a hidden power to alter how a person is treated – how she acts and what she does – thereby even what she thinks or feels. As Rachel, reflecting back on her first days in primary school said: 'It was so embarrassing, I didn't know. I didn't know where anything was or should be, I didn't know the teacher, and my friends from nursery were in the other class' (Dunlop, 2002a).

The disharmony described by Kienig, and the need for transition activities (Bröstrom, Margetts) to support the adaptation or problem solving capacities (Fabian, 2002) of children in transition are resonant of Weisner's idea of the 'ecological niche', or 'activity setting' (Edwards, 2001: 5). We can see transition activities as day-to-day experiences which provide children with opportunities to learn and develop in the company of others. The nature of transition activities might allow children the chance to engage in such activities in peer groups, with older and differently experienced children already in elementary education, or indeed with the various adults who populate their lives (Dunlop, 2002a). Further we want to emphasise the essential contribution of parents in that process (Griebel and Niesel, Johansson): parents' values, beliefs, and socio-economic status, as well as their experience of education will effect how families live (Goodnow,

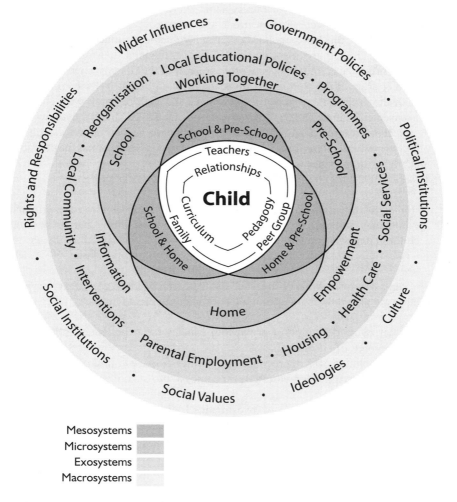

Mesosystems
Microsystems
Exosystems
Macrosystems

Figure 12.1 A transition systems approach

2001), and the kinds of family transitions which their children will experience (Fthenakis, 1998).

The resilience, versatility and promise of young children as evidenced in their capacity to adapt to, to tolerate and especially contribute to the creation and the co-construction, of the systems in which they live, grow and learn is central to any enquiry about educational transitions. So, too, is the understanding that public policy has the power to affect the well-being and development of children by determining the conditions of their lives. These other structural forms merge with the interaction of each of our conceptual levels to create an interrelationship with the childhoods at the centre of our system. There is, as Peters points out, an increasingly complex web of connections to be made.

As researchers, this has demanded of us an involvement with children, we have been party to their transitions, and may have influenced them. The effect of researcher presence at transition is twofold at least. In the first place we sought the informed consent of the children involved and of their parents (Greig and Taylor, 1999), in the second there is a justifiable need for such research with children (Christensen and James, 2000). There has been a need to establish the knowledge base and then to move from contextualising what we and others have seen, to developing new paradigms for transition, and to ask if this makes or has the potential to make transitions better for children.

Clarke (1992), highlighting transition as a research issue, wrote:

> studies of transition have shown that for some young children the primary school may provide a less stimulating and challenging setting than these same children experienced at the pre-school.
>
> (Clarke, 1992: 10)

We can ask why is this still an issue? Our research makes it clear that it is, and that there are also new challenges which are likely to create hurdles:

- the increasing definition of pre-school educational experiences through the development of curriculum;
- the implications of a significant political investment of public funding;
- increased demands for measurable outcomes of pre-school experience in some countries;
- a consideration of pre-school investment's longer term success; and
- an impetus to provide a more integrated early years experience (Moss, 2001), but nevertheless a distinctive one (Kagan, 2001).

In this climate of fast moving change in early years education it is widely accepted, and government documents increasingly promote, the importance of continuity and progression in transition as key elements in subsequent school success. We have added that they are also key elements in the present, here-and-now experience of children.

The more fluid transitions that occur in the home educator perspective (Fortune-Wood), the open acknowledgement of independence and autonomy, and consequently of confidence, highlight how institutionalised systems are powerful, and promote induction into a particular form of culture, but that the cultures in each sector of early education may still be poles apart. As Neuman shows in Chapter 1 of this book, if we strive for the distinctiveness of both early childhood and early schooling, each must be recognised as equal and important partners. Even within our set of nested systems, we have to acknowledge the gaps, bridge them and begin to narrow them.

Following on from this it may then be possible to consider a transitional curriculum with shared ventures for pre-school and school children; transitional settings in which children's present independence and responsibility is supported and used to smooth induction into the new; transitional relationships where children know their new teachers before they join them but where maintaining previous relationships is valued, and transitional teaching and learning contexts where new and more demanding challenges are offered through a recognisable pedagogy. Finally we embrace the vital importance of recognising the challenge of being a transitional child, as new identities and roles are taken on. As the new world of day-care, pre-school or school becomes familiar and more predictable, the child's agency and competence will then be confirmed.

We need to go further still. We need to ask children and enlist their help in what new children need to know. We need to make room for them, along with their families and friends, to co-construct this particular educational transition. Then we might be able to learn from home educators and be able to engender intrinsic, self-directed transitions rather than pre-ordained ones (Fortune-Wood).

We have asserted the importance of an appropriate pedagogy, of a reconciliation of two different traditions (Neuman and Peters), of an acknowledgment of varied perspectives, of the child's voice and the family involvement. The present significance of our studies of children at a transition phase of early educational experience is reinforced by the recognition of new transitions in childhood itself as our social systems, social formations and social imperatives change.

We can conclude that each and every aspect of transition, continuity and progression in the early years is complex, should be debated, reflected upon and researched. There are no simple solutions, rather there are opportunities for communities to work together, to resist the artificial boundaries that educational structures, different philosophies, different curricula and quite varied views of the contribution that parents can and may make, impose on us. Maybe then it might be possible to replace the transition model of schooling with one which espouses difference, doesn't push for sameness, values independence and builds on it, and develops a continuity model, in which educators, children and parents together form a local pattern of transition which suits their present culture.

References

Bronfenbrenner, U. (1979) *The Ecology of Human Development: Experiments by Nature and Design*. Cambridge and London: Harvard University Press.

Bronfenbrenner, U. (1989) 'Ecological systems theory'. In R. Vasta (ed.) (1992) *Theories of Child Development: Revised Formulations and Current Issues*. London: Jessica Kingsley

Burman, E. (1994) *Deconstructing Developmental Psychology*. London: Routledge.

Christensen, P. and James, A. (2000) *Research with Children: Perspectives and Practices*. London: Falmer Press

Clarke, M. (1992) 'Early education'. In *Reflections on Curriculum Issues*. Dundee: SCCC.

Davies, B. (1982) *Life in the Classroom and Playground*. London: Routledge and Kegan Paul.

Dunlop, A.W.A. (2002a) *Transition Guidelines for Stirling Council Early Years Service*. Forthcoming.

Dunlop, A.W.A (2002b) 'A study into continuity and progression for young children in early educational transitions'. Unpublished PhD thesis, University of Strathclyde, Glasgow.

Edwards, C.P. (2001) 'Parental ethnotheories of child development: the american perspective'. Paper prepared for the International Workshop on Scientific Advances in Indigenous Psychologies. Taiwan. 29 October–1 November.

Fabian, H. (2002) *Children Starting School. A Guide to Successful Transitions and Transfers for Teachers and Assistants*. London: David Fulton.

Fthenakis, W.E. (1998) 'Family transitions and quality in early childhood education', *European Early Childhood Education Research Journal* 6(1), 5–18.

Goodnow, J. (2001) 'Commentary: culture and parenting, cross cutting issues'. *International Society for the Study of Behavioral Development Newsletter* 1(38), 13–14.

Greig, A. and Taylor, J. (1999) *Doing Research with Children*. London: Sage.

HMI (2001) *Early Intervention, 1998–2000*. A report by HM Inspectorate of Education. Edinburgh: The Stationary Office and http://www.scotland.gov.uk/hmie.

James, A., Jenks, C. and Prout, A. (1998) *Theorising Childhood*. Cambridge: Polity Press.

Jenks, C. (1996) 'The postmodern child'. In Brannen, J. and O'Brien, M. (eds), *Children in Families: Research and Policy*. London: Falmer Press.

Kagan, S.L. (2001) 'Summarising the reports of the working groups'. OECD Conference reporting the Thematic Review of Early Education and Care in 12 European Countries. Stockholm, 13–15 June.

Mayall, B. (ed.) (1994) *Children's Childhoods: Observed and Experienced*. London: Falmer.

Moss, P. (2001) 'Beyond early childhood education and care'. Paper presented at the OECD Conference reporting the Thematic Review of Early Education and Care in 12 European Countries. Stockholm, 13–15 June.

Pollard, A. (1985) *The Social World of the Primary School*. London: Cassell.

Pollard, A. and Filer, A. (1996) *The Social World of Children's Learning*. London: Cassell.

Prout, A. (2000) 'Children's participation: control and self-realisation in British late modernity'. *Children in Society* 14, 304–15.

Van Gennep, A. (1960) *The Rites of Passage* (1908). London: Routledge and Kegan Paul.

Further reading

Asher S.R. and Gottman J.M. (eds) (1981) *The Development of Children's Friendships*. Cambridge: Cambridge University Press.

Ball, C. (1994) *Start Right: The Importance of Early Learning*. London: The Royal Society for the Encouragement of Arts, Manufactures and Commerce.

Barbour, N.H. and Seefeldt, C. (1993) *Developmental Continuity Across Preschool and Primary Grades. Implications for Teachers*. Wheaton, MD: Association for Childhood Education International.

Barrett, G. (1986) *Starting School: An Evaluation of the Experience*. London: Assistant Masters and Mistresses Association.

Bastiani, J. and Doyle, N. (1994) *Home and School: Building a Better Partnership*. London: National Consumer Council.

Bastiani, J. and Wolfendale, S. (eds) (1996) *Home-School Work in Britain*. London: David Fulton Publishers.

Bennet, C. and Downes, P. (1998) 'Leading parents to fuller involvement', *Management in Education* 12(5), 12–14.

Bennett, N. and Kell, J. (1989) *A Good Start? Four Year Olds in Infant Schools*. Oxford: Basil Blackwell.

Bernard Van Leer Foundation (1993) 'Transition', *Bernard Van Leer Foundation Newsletter* 70, 1–13.

Bredekamp, S. (ed.) (1987) *Developmentally Appropriate Practice in Early Childhood Programs Serving Children From Birth Through Age 8*. Washington DC: National Association for the Education of Young Children.

Brown, S. and Cleave, S. (1994) *Four Year Olds in School: Quality Matters*, 2nd Edition. Slough: NFER.

Bruner, J.S. (1996) 'What we have Learned about Early Learning', *European Early Childhood Education Research Journal* 4(1), 5–16.

Burrell, A. and Bubb, S. (2000) 'Teacher feedback in the reception class: associations with children's positive adjustment to school', *Education 3–13* 28(3), 58–69.

Campbell, C. (2000) 'Our children start school too early', *Early Years Educator* 2(7), 3– 4.

Campbell Clark, S. (2000) 'Work/family border theory: a new theory of work/family balance', *Human Relations* 53(6), 747–70.

Cleave, S. and Brown, S. (1989) *Four Year Olds in School: Meeting Their Needs*. Slough: National Foundation for Educational Research.

Cleave, S., Jowett, S. and Bate, M. (1982) *... And So To School: A Study of Continuity from Pre-school to Infant School*. Berkshire: NFER-Nelson.

Cousins, J. (1990) 'Are your little Humpty Dumpties floating or sinking? What sense do children of four make of reception class at school? Different conceptions at the time of transition', *Early Years* 10(2), 28–38.

Crnic, K. and Lamberty, G. (1994). 'Reconsidering school readiness: conceptual and applied perspectives', *Early Education and Development* 5(2). Available online http://readyweb.crc.uiic.edu/library/1994/crcnic1.html

Crosser, S.L. (1991) 'Summer birth date children: kindergarten entrance age and academic achievement', *Journal of Educational Research* 84(3), 140–6.

Dalli, C. (1999) 'Learning to be in childcare: mothers' stories of their child's "settling-in"', *European Early Childhood Education Research Journal* 7(2), 53–66.

David, T. (1990) *Under Five – Under Educated?* Milton Keynes: Open University Press.

Davie, R. and. Galloway, D. (eds) (1996) *Listening to Children in Education*. London: David Fulton.

Deegan, J.G. (1996) *Children's Friendships in Culturally Diverse Classrooms*. London: Falmer Press.

Department of Education Northern Ireland (2000) 'From pre-school to school: a review of the research literature', *Research Briefing 3/2000*. Bangor, Co Down: Statistics and Research Agency and Department of Education.

Dockett, S., Perry, R. and Tracey, D. (1997) 'Getting ready for school'. Paper presented at the Australian Association for Research in Education Annual Conference, Brisbane.

Edgar, D. (1986) 'Family background and the transition to school'. *Primary Education*, 17(4), 16–21.

Fabian, H. (1996) 'Children starting school: parents in partnership', *Mentoring and Tutoring* 4(1), 12–22.

Fabian, H. (2000) 'Small steps to starting school', *International Journal of Early Years Education* 8(2), 141–53.

Fieldhouse, J. (1988) 'Going to school', *Management in Education* 2(4), 28–9.

Galton, M., Gray, J. and Rudduck, J. (1999) *The Impact of School Transitions and Transfers on Pupil Progress and Attainment: Research Report RR131*. London: DfEE, HMSO.

Gregory, E. and Biarnes, J. (1994) 'Tony and Jean-Francois looking for sense in the strangeness of school'. In H. Dombey and M. Meek Spencer (eds), *First Steps Together*. Stoke-on-Trent: Trentham Books.

Hallgarten, J. (2000) 'Involving the parents: parent–school relationships', *Education Journal* 50, 10–11.

Harkness, S. and Super, C.M. (1994) 'Parental ethnotheories in culture and human development', *Researching Early Childhood* 2(1), 59–84.

Holliday, B. (2001) 'Is school always the best way to start?', *Early Years Educator* 2(9) 6–7.

Education and Employment Committee (Education Sub-Committee) (2001) *Government's Response to the First Report from the Committee Session 2000–2001: Early Years*. London: The Stationery Office.

Hughes, M., Pinkerton, G. and Plewis, I. (1979) 'Children's difficulties on starting infant school', *Journal of Child Psychology and Psychiatry* 20, 187–96.

Hughes, M., Wikeley, F. and Nash, T. (1994) *Parents and their Children's Schools*. Oxford: Blackwell Publishers.

Itskowitz, R., Strauss, H., and Fruchter, D. (1987) 'Does familiarity with school increase adjustment?', *School Psychology International* 8(4), 251–5.

James, A. and Prout, A. (1997) 'Re-presenting childhood: time and transition in the study of childhood'. In A. James and A. Prout (eds), *Constructing and Reconstructing Childhood: Contemporary Issues in the Sociological Study of Childhood*, 2nd edition. London: Falmer Press.

Kontos, S. and Wilcox-Herzog, A. (1997) 'Influences on children's competence in early childhood classrooms', *Early Childhood Research Quarterly* 12, 247–62.

Lombardi, J. (1992) 'Beyond transition: ensuring continuity in early childhood services', *ERIC Digest*. Champaign: University of Illinois.

Margetts, K. (1999) 'Transition to school: Te raranga I te oranga tangata'. *Proceedings of the Seventh Early Childhood Convention, Nelson, New Zealand, Sept 27–30, 1999*, Vol 2, 229 36.

Marshall, P. (1988) *Transition and Continuity in the Educational Process*. London: Kogan Page.

Morrison, I. (2000) '"School's great – apart from the lessons": sustaining the excitement of learning post-transfer', *Improving Schools* 3(1), 46–9.

Moss, P. and Pence, A. (eds) (1994) *Valuing Quality in Early Childhood Services*. London: Paul Chapman Publishing.

National Foundation for Educational Research/School Curriculum Development Committee (1987) *Four-Year-Olds in School: Policy and Practice*. Slough: NFER/SCDC.

Osgood, J. and Sharp, C. (2000) *Developing Early Education and Childcare Services for the 21st Century*. Slough: The National Foundation for Educational Research.

Ouston, J. and Hood, S. (2000) *Home–School Agreements: A True Partnership?* London: The Research and Information on State Education Trust (RISE).

Pascal, C. (1990) *Under-Fives in the Infant Classroom*. Stoke-on-Trent: Trentham Books.

Pedersen, E., Faucher, T.A. and Eaton, W.W. (1978) 'A new perspective on the effects of first-grade teachers on children's subsequent adult status', *Harvard Educational Review* 48, 1–31.

Pugh, G. (1996) 'Four-year-olds in school: what is appropriate provision?', *Children UK*. National Children's Bureau. Winter Issue 11.

Robson, S. (1996) 'Home and school: a potentially powerful partnership'. In Robson, S. and Smedley, S. (eds), *Education in Early Childhood*. London: David Fulton Publishers.

Rudduck, J. (1996) 'Going to "the big school": the turbulence of transition'. In Rudduck, J., Chaplain, R. and Wallace, G. (eds), *School Improvement: What Can Pupils Tell Us?* London: David Fulton.

Office of Educational Research and Improvement (1992) South Eastern Regional Vision for Education (SERVE). A resource booklet on transition: SERVEing Young Children Project (Report No. RP91002010). Washington, DC: Office of Educational Research and Improvement. (ERIC Document Reproduction Service No. ED 357892).

Sharp, C. (1995) *School Entry and the Impact of Season of Birth on Attainment.* Slough: NFER Research.

Sharp, P. (2001) *Nurturing Emotional Literacy*. London: David Fulton.

Stelling, C. and Fabian, H. (1996) 'An Open Door', *Child Education* 73(1), 54–5.

Tudge, J., Shanahan, M.J. and Valsiner, J. (eds) (1997) *Comparisons in Human Development: Understanding Time and Context*. Cambridge: Cambridge University Press.

Waterland, L. (1994) *Not a Perfect Offering: A New School Year.* Gloucester: The Thimble Press.

Willes, M.J. (1983) *Children Into Pupils*. London: Routledge and Kegan Paul.

Index